Your Ego Is Your Biggest Downfall

How to Recognize, Overcome, and Rise Above It

By: Bridgette Gajadhar

Your Ego Is Your Biggest Downfall
How to Recognize, Overcome, and Rise Above It
by Bridgette Gajadhar

Published by Pons Veritas™
ISBN: 978-1-968471-02-6
www.ponsveritas.com

Disclaimer

For permissions, inquiries, or more information, contact: ponsveritas@gmail.com

First Edition: 2025

Table of Contents

Introduction: The Illusion of Ego

You hear the word "ego" tossed around all the time—usually as an insult.

"That person has such a big ego."

"They let their ego ruin everything."

"Check your ego at the door."

It's got a bad reputation, and for good reason. Ego is the force that keeps people trapped in cycles of insecurity, competition, and self-sabotage. It's the voice in your head that tells you you're not good enough—until the moment it flips and tells you you're better than everyone else. It's the fragile foundation people build their entire identity on, only to watch it crumble under the weight of reality. But here's the thing: **ego isn't the enemy. It's just misunderstood.**

What Is Ego? (And What It Isn't.)

Ego is not self-love. It's not confidence. It's not even about being selfish or arrogant. Ego is the mask you wear, the identity you cling to, the part of you that constantly seeks validation, protection, or control.

The ego is the middleman between who you **really are** and who you **think you need to be** to survive in this world. It's not inherently bad—it's just trying to do its job, keeping you safe by maintaining a sense of identity. But the problem is, **most people don't realize how much of their life is run by their ego.**

Self-Confidence vs. Ego-Driven Identity

There's a fine line between **true confidence** and an **ego-driven identity**—and knowing the difference changes everything.

- **Confidence** comes from inner trust. It doesn't need approval. It doesn't need to be the loudest in the room. It just *is*.
- **Ego** thrives on external validation. It constantly compares, competes, and reacts. It builds an identity around status, appearance, and control, but it's never satisfied.

Ego makes you **defensive**, confidence makes you **secure**.
Ego seeks **dominance**, confidence seeks **growth**.
Ego fears **losing**, confidence knows **there's nothing to prove**.
The more you let your ego run the show, the more you limit yourself without even realizing it.

How Ego Can Control Your Life Without You Even Realizing It

Ego is sneaky. It doesn't announce itself loudly—it operates in the background, shaping your thoughts, choices, and reactions. It's why people stay in toxic relationships out of pride. It's why people chase success for the wrong reasons and feel empty when they get it. It's why small criticisms feel like personal attacks.

If you've ever:

- Felt the need to prove yourself constantly
- Reacted defensively instead of listening
- Stayed in situations just to "win"
- Held grudges that drained your energy
- Felt insecure despite external success

Then congratulations—your ego has been running the show. And you're not alone. **Everyone has an ego. The question is, are you controlling it, or is it controlling you?**

The Silent Killer of Happiness, Success, and Relationships

Ego is the ultimate trickster. It convinces you that its way is the only way, that you're right, that you're justified, that you need to prove something. And in doing so, it quietly kills your happiness, your growth, and your ability to connect with others.

- **In relationships** – Ego creates conflict, misunderstandings, and prideful standoffs. It makes people hold onto anger just to avoid admitting they were wrong.
- **In success** – Ego makes you chase external rewards instead of internal fulfillment. It keeps you stuck in cycles of proving yourself instead of actually enjoying what you do.
- **In personal growth** – Ego tells you that you already "know everything," keeping you from learning, evolving, and expanding.

The good news? **You don't need to destroy your ego. You just need to master it.**

The Goal of This Book

This book isn't about telling you to erase your ego. That's impossible. Ego will always be part of you. But what you *can* do is understand it, work with it, and make sure it's not driving your life off a cliff.

The key is to **make your ego work for you, not against you.** Instead of letting it sabotage your success, you can learn how to use it as a tool—to push yourself forward without letting it run wild.

By the end of this book, you'll learn:

- How to recognize when your ego is controlling you
- How to shift from ego-driven reactions to conscious decisions
- How to build true confidence that doesn't need external validation
- How to have better relationships by leaving ego out of the conversation
- How to achieve success that actually fulfills you

Mastering your ego doesn't mean losing yourself—it means **finding your real self underneath all the noise.** And once you do that? **Everything changes.**

A Short Quiz: "How Much is Your Ego Controlling You?"

Instructions:
Answer the following questions honestly.
Keep track of how many times you answer **YES**.

1. How Do You Handle Criticism?

☐ Do you get defensive when someone critiques you?

☐ Do you dismiss feedback instead of considering if it might be true?

☐ Do you find it hard to admit when you're wrong?

2. How Do You See Yourself vs. Others?

☐ Do you often feel like people are against you or don't understand you?

☐ Do you compare yourself to others and feel superior or inferior?

☐ Do you feel like you have to prove your worth in conversations, relationships, or work?

3. How Do You Handle Success & Failure?

☐ Do you take full credit for your wins but blame external factors for your failures?

☐ Do you feel threatened when someone else succeeds?

☐ Do you ignore advice from people who are more experienced than you?

4. How Do You Approach Conversations & Conflicts?

☐ Do you always feel the need to "win" arguments?

☐ Do you find it hard to truly listen without planning your response?

☐ Do you hold grudges because admitting fault feels like losing?

Scoring & Interpretation:

0-3 YES Answers: Your ego is under control. You have a strong sense of self-awareness and humility. Keep growing!

4-7 YES Answers: Your ego has some control over you, but you're self-aware enough to start shifting it. Pay attention to the areas where you struggle the most.

8-12 YES Answers: Your ego is running the show. But the good news? **You're reading this book—so you're already on the path to mastering it.**

Part 1: The Self-Sabotage Trap

How Ego is Your Own Worst Enemy

Let's get one thing straight: the ego isn't evil. It's just loud, scared, and obsessed with control. It's the voice in your head that wants to protect you—but ends up keeping you stuck. It's the reason you lash out, shut down, overthink, chase validation, or play small. The ego says, *"Don't change, it's not safe."* Meanwhile, your highest self is whispering, *"But we can do better."*

This part of the book is about exposing your ego for what it really is: a false sense of self that thrives on fear, pride, and insecurity. It wears masks, creates stories, and convinces you that protecting your image is more important than healing your soul.

We're going to break down exactly how ego shows up in your daily life—and how it secretly sabotages your growth, happiness, and peace. But don't worry, we're not here to shame you. We're here to wake you up, call you out (with love), and get you *free*.

Ready to meet the real enemy? Spoiler: it's not them. It's not life. It's not your past.

It's the version of you that's too scared to let go.

Let's fix that.

Chapter 1: The Addictive Illusion of Ego

Ego feels *good*. It feels powerful. It feels like confidence, security, and control. It's the little voice in your head that tells you, *"I know what I'm doing. I don't need to listen to anyone. I'm right."*

And that's exactly how it keeps you trapped.

Ego is the ultimate illusion—it makes you believe it's working in your favor while secretly keeping you stuck. It convinces you that standing your ground, never admitting fault, and refusing to change is strength. But in reality, it's a cage disguised as armor. It whispers reassurance, feeding you the comforting lie that you've already got it all figured out, when in truth, that very mindset is what holds you back from growth, understanding, and deeper fulfillment.

It's like a sugar high: an instant rush of validation, a boost of superiority, a fleeting sense of control. But just like any high, the crash always comes. The frustration of stagnation. The resentment that builds when things don't go your way. The quiet moments when you realize that, despite always feeling "right," you're not truly happy, and you don't feel as secure as you thought.

The hardest part? Ego is addictive. It feeds on pride, on the need to be seen as strong, on the fear of vulnerability. And just like any addiction, the first step to breaking free is realizing how much control it actually has over you. Because the moment you acknowledge its grip, you take back your power. True confidence, true security, and true control don't come from ego—they come from the willingness to grow beyond it.

Why Ego Feels Good (But Is Actually Self-Destructive)

When your ego is in charge, you feel untouchable.

- You don't second-guess yourself.
- You don't feel insecure.
- You feel like you have something to prove -and you're proving it.

It's an intoxicating feeling, like standing on top of the world, completely sure of yourself. Ego makes you feel *right*, and being right feels good. It gives you a sense of superiority, a sense of purpose, a sense of certainty in a world that often feels chaotic and unpredictable.

But here's the truth: ego feeds off illusions, not reality.

- It makes you feel confident—but only as long as you're being praised.
- It makes you feel in control—but only as long as you're not challenged.
- It makes you feel secure—but only as long as nothing threatens your self-image.

Ego is a house of cards. The second something shakes that illusion—whether it's criticism, failure, or someone disagreeing with you—ego goes into full meltdown mode. That's when the cracks start to show:

- You get defensive, shutting down any perspective that doesn't align with yours.
- You get angry, lashing out instead of listening.

- You feel insecure, but instead of addressing it, you mask it with arrogance.
- You take things personally, even when they aren't about you.

Because ego doesn't build *real* confidence—it builds a fragile, paper-thin version that constantly needs reinforcement.

- If no one is clapping for you, ego whispers that you're losing.
- If someone questions you, ego screams that you have to prove them wrong at all costs.
- If you fail, ego convinces you to either deny it completely or drown in self-loathing.

And if you don't recognize that pattern, you'll spend your entire life feeding your ego while starving your true self.

- You'll chase validation instead of wisdom.
- You'll choose being right over being happy.
- You'll build a life that looks strong on the outside but feels hollow on the inside.

Because ego's greatest trick is making you believe it's protecting you—when in reality, it's the very thing holding you back.

How Ego Tricks You Into Thinking You're Right (When You're Actually Stuck)

Ego has one main goal: **to be right.**

- It doesn't care if you're actually making the best choices.
- It doesn't care if your actions are helping or hurting you.

- It just wants to *feel* right—even if that means keeping you stuck in toxic patterns.

Ever been in a situation where you *knew* you were wrong, but still refused to admit it? That's ego.
- You hold onto a grudge because letting it go would mean admitting you overreacted.
- You double down on a bad decision because changing course would mean acknowledging a mistake.
- You dismiss someone's advice because accepting it would mean admitting you didn't have all the answers.

Ego convinces you that backing down is weakness, that changing your mind is failure, that listening to others somehow makes you less capable. It's a defense mechanism, a way to protect your sense of self—because if you're always right, you never have to feel embarrassed, uncertain, or vulnerable.

But here's the irony: **ego makes you defend the very things that hold you back.** Instead of learning, growing, and improving, you stay trapped in cycles that don't serve you.
- You push people away rather than admitting you need help.
- You refuse to acknowledge when something isn't working, prolonging your own struggles.
- You waste energy proving a point instead of finding real solutions.

And the worst part? Ego makes this *feel* like the right thing to do. It keeps you comfortable—wrapped in the safety of self-righteousness, protected from the discomfort of growth.

But comfort isn't always a good thing. Sometimes, **comfort is the enemy of progress.**

The moment you stop needing to be right all the time is the moment you actually start winning.

- When you let go of the need to prove yourself, you open the door to real self-improvement.
- When you embrace humility, you gain wisdom instead of wasting time defending your mistakes.
- When you stop fighting for an illusion of control, you gain actual control over your choices, your growth, and your future.

Because real confidence doesn't come from *always* being right—it comes from being open enough to learn, evolve, and get better every single day.

The Cycle of Defensiveness, Self-Justification, and Pride

Ego loves a good cycle—and the most dangerous one looks like this:

1. Defensiveness

Someone challenges you, gives feedback, or offers a different perspective. Instead of listening, ego makes you feel **attacked.** You feel the immediate urge to protect yourself, even if the person isn't trying to harm you. Your mind races to shut them down, to prove they don't understand, to make sure they don't "win."

2. Self-Justification

Now, you start listing all the reasons you're *right*. Maybe you bring up past experiences that justify your reaction. Maybe you twist the situation to make it seem like the other person is wrong, not you. Even if a small part of you recognizes that you might be off base, ego drowns that voice out, convincing you to **double down instead of reflect.**

3. Pride

At this point, you're invested in your own argument. **Backing down would feel like losing.** But instead of asking yourself if you even *want* to win this argument, ego keeps pushing you forward. You've built an identity around being right, and admitting otherwise feels like tearing a piece of yourself away. So, you dig in deeper. You defend harder. You reject any perspective that doesn't align with yours.

And just like that, you're trapped in the cycle.

The more you repeat this pattern, the harder it becomes to break. Over time, ego **trains you to resist change, even when change is the only thing that can set you free.** Instead of growing, you stay stuck in a loop where being right matters more than being happy, fulfilled, or at peace.

So how do you break out?

- **Pause before reacting.** When someone challenges you, take a breath. Ask yourself: *Am I listening, or am I just waiting to defend myself?*

- **Separate ego from truth.** Just because you feel attacked doesn't mean you *are* being attacked. Just because someone disagrees with you doesn't mean they're against you.

- **Get curious instead of combative.** Instead of shutting someone down, ask them why they see things the way they do. You don't have to agree, but you *can* learn something.

- **Detach from the need to "win."** Ask yourself: *Do I want to be right, or do I want to grow?*

Breaking the cycle doesn't mean you're weak—it means you're strong enough to evolve. And that's where real power lies.

The Wake-Up Call: Recognizing When Ego Is Holding You Back

If you've ever:

- **Gotten defensive** over something small, even when it didn't really matter

- **Argued** just for the sake of being right, not because it was actually important

- **Rejected help or advice** that could have actually benefited you, just to prove you could do it on your own

- **Held onto anger or resentment** because you didn't want to be the first to let go, even when it was exhausting
- **Stayed in a situation longer than you should have** just because walking away felt like "losing"

Then congratulations—your ego has been running the show.

Ego doesn't announce itself. It disguises its grip as **strength, confidence, and control.** It makes you believe you're protecting yourself when, in reality, you're **blocking your own growth.** It whispers that letting go means giving up, that changing your mind means admitting weakness, and that seeking help makes you less capable. But these are all illusions—traps designed to keep you stuck.

But here's the thing: **once you recognize the pattern, you can break it.**

- Instead of getting **defensive**, pause and ask yourself: *"Am I reacting out of pride or out of logic?"* When someone challenges you, is your first instinct to listen or to argue? Do you actually disagree, or are you just resisting being questioned?
- Instead of **self-justifying**, ask yourself: *"Am I trying to be right, or am I trying to be better?"* Are you holding onto your stance because it truly serves you, or because you just don't want to back down?
- Instead of **holding onto pride**, remind yourself: *"Real strength is in growth, not in proving a point."* Being "right" won't always make you happy, but learning and evolving will.

The moment you shift from **reacting** to **reflecting**, ego loses its power.

- You stop arguing just to win and start **listening to understand.**
- You stop rejecting help and start **allowing yourself to grow.**
- You stop fearing change and start **embracing the freedom of evolving.**

And most importantly, you stop seeing everything as a battle to win or lose. **You realize that life isn't about proving yourself—it's about improving yourself.**

Because at the end of the day, **ego only wins if you let it.** But when you choose self-awareness over self-defense, reflection over reaction, and growth over stubbornness, **you win in a way that actually matters.**

Ego Isn't the Enemy—It's the Alarm

Here's the truth most people miss:

Ego isn't evil. It's just scared.

Ego's job is to protect you. It shows up when something feels uncertain, unsafe, or out of your control. The problem isn't that ego exists—it's what happens when you let it run the show without checking where it's coming from.

Ego doesn't scream for no reason. It's trying to protect something—your image, your sense of security, your pride. But it often does so by choosing defensiveness over growth, control over connection, and pride over peace.

That's why ego isn't your enemy—it's your **alarm system**.

It's the internal fire alarm that goes off anytime your identity feels threatened.

And just like a real alarm, it's not always accurate. Sometimes, it's reacting to smoke, not fire.

But the alarm still matters.

So instead of silencing it or letting it take over, pause and **ask what it's trying to protect.**

The Reframe:

Ego says: "They don't respect me."

But the deeper truth might be: *"I don't feel heard."*

Ego says: "I'm not apologizing—I didn't do anything wrong."

But the deeper truth might be: *"I'm afraid that admitting fault makes me weak."*

Ego says: "I'm fine on my own. I don't need help."

But the deeper truth might be: *"I don't want to feel vulnerable or dependent."*

The goal isn't to destroy ego—it's to decode it.

Use ego as your internal signal.

Whenever you feel defensive, offended, or reactive—pause.

Instead of asking, *"How do I defend myself?"* ask:

"What is my ego trying to protect right now?"

And then lead yourself from truth—not from fear.

The 3 Flavors of Ego—Which One Runs You Most?

Ego doesn't always show up the same way for everyone. It has different masks—and the more self-aware you are about which one you wear, the faster you can take it off.

Here are the three most common ego styles:

1. The Performer

Craves: *Praise, admiration, recognition*

Fears: *Being overlooked or irrelevant*

How it shows up:

- Constantly needing validation and attention
- Measuring self-worth by how "impressive" you look
- Struggling when you're not being celebrated

Underneath it all:

This ego is fueled by the fear that *being enough* depends on how much you're seen or applauded.

The truth:

You're valuable even when no one's clapping. You don't need to perform to be worthy.

2. The Protector

Craves: *Respect, control, independence*

Fears: *Vulnerability, emotional exposure*

How it shows up:

- Brushing off feelings or conflict
- Acting unbothered when you're actually hurt
- Avoiding deep conversations or emotional intimacy

Underneath it all:

This ego thinks being strong means never needing help or showing softness.

The truth:

True strength isn't in hiding emotion—it's in being real and safe within yourself.

3. The Prover

Craves: *Being right, being the best, being "above" others*

Fears: *Being seen as wrong, uncertain, or average*

How it shows up:

- Needing to win every argument
- Talking over people or dismissing their ideas
- Getting defensive when challenged

Underneath it all:

This ego believes your value depends on how much smarter, better, or more capable you appear.

The truth:

You don't need to outdo others to have worth. Growth is about getting better—not being the best.

Quick Check-In: Which ego style shows up most for you?

The Performer

The Protector

The Prover

Now ask:

What fear is it trying to shield me from?

What would happen if I stopped feeding it—and started listening instead?

Exercise: Spot the Ego – Awareness Audit

This exercise is designed to help you recognize how ego shows up in your day-to-day life—and begin shifting from automatic reactions to conscious reflection.

Step 1: Real-Life Reflection

Think of a moment in the past week where you felt frustrated, defensive, or misunderstood.

What happened? (brief description)

How did you react in the moment?

What did your ego tell you? (e.g., "They don't get it," "I'm right," "I shouldn't have to explain myself.")

Step 2: Ego Pattern Recognition

Check off any ego-driven thoughts or behaviors you experienced during that moment:

I felt the need to be right

I shut down instead of staying open

I rejected advice or feedback

I took something personally that wasn't meant that way

I got defensive instead of curious

I reacted emotionally instead of pausing to reflect

I made the moment about me instead of listening

Which one stood out the most—and why?

Step 3: The Reframe

Now, let's shift the lens. Imagine going through that same situation without ego leading the way.

What would a grounded, self-aware version of you do differently?

What might you have learned or understood better if you were listening, not defending?

What would the outcome have been if you responded instead of reacted?

Step 4: Your Ego Awareness Mantra

Choose one—or write your own:

- "I don't need to be right—I want to be real."
- "My ego doesn't define me. My growth does."
- "Pause. Reflect. Respond."
- "I'm not here to prove myself—I'm here to improve myself."
- "Comfort keeps me stuck. Awareness sets me free."

Final Thoughts: The First Step to Mastering Ego

Ego is like a shadow—it follows you everywhere. It's always present, influencing your thoughts, decisions, and reactions. But the more aware of it you become, the less control it has over you.

The goal isn't to **eliminate** ego. That's impossible. Ego is a natural part of being human. It gives us drive, ambition, and a sense of identity. The problem isn't that ego exists—the problem is when it runs the show unchecked, keeping you trapped in defensiveness, pride, and stagnation.

The real power comes in **understanding ego**—recognizing when it's helping you and when it's holding you back. Instead of letting it control you, you learn how to control *it*. You shift from reacting impulsively to responding with awareness. You move from chasing validation to building true confidence. You stop seeing every challenge as a threat and start using them as opportunities for growth.

Mastering ego isn't about suppression—it's about **balance.** It's about knowing when to stand your ground and when to let go. When to trust yourself and when to stay open to new perspectives. When to speak and when to listen.

Chapter 2: How Ego Blinds You from Reality

Ego is like a bad pair of prescription glasses—it distorts everything you see, but because you've been wearing them for so long, you don't even realize it. It warps reality, making neutral situations feel like personal attacks. A small misunderstanding suddenly feels like betrayal. A simple disagreement turns into proof that someone is against you.

And the worst part? Ego doesn't just change how you see the present—it rewrites the past, too. It makes you the victim when you need sympathy, the hero when you need validation, the one who was always right when you don't want to admit otherwise. It feeds you a version of events that protects your pride, even if that version isn't entirely true.

But here's the problem: when your perception is distorted, your decisions will be too. You react to illusions, not reality. You hold grudges over things that were never meant to hurt you. You cut people off for offenses they never actually committed. You stay stuck in a loop where your own assumptions and insecurities dictate how you experience life, and instead of questioning it, you just keep reinforcing the same narrative.

It's exhausting, isn't it? The constant need to defend, to prove, to justify. The endless cycle of feeling misunderstood, unappreciated, or wronged. But what if the issue isn't what's happening around you—what if it's the way you're seeing it?

The good news is, once you realize how ego distorts reality, you can start breaking free. Instead of assuming, you start asking. Instead of reacting, you start observing. Instead of replaying the same story, you start questioning if the story is even true. And that's when things get real—because seeing clearly means finally stepping out of the illusion ego has kept you trapped in.

Ego Distorts Situations by Making Everything Feel Personal

Ever had someone cancel plans on you, and instead of thinking, *Maybe they're busy,* you immediately felt rejected?
Ever had someone give you feedback, and instead of hearing it as helpful, you took it as a personal attack?

That's ego.

Ego makes everything feel like it's about *you*. It convinces you that people's actions are direct reflections of how they feel about you—even when they have nothing to do with you at all. It takes neutral events and twists them into personal narratives. Suddenly, you're not just dealing with what's happening—you're dealing with the *story* your ego has created about it.

Your friend didn't text back?

Ego says, *They must not care about me.*

Reality? They might be dealing with something in their own life, lost in thought, or simply didn't see the message yet.

Your coworker disagrees with you in a meeting?

Ego says, *They're trying to undermine me.*

Reality? They might just see the situation differently, and their input isn't about *you*, but about the topic at hand.

Someone else succeeds in an area you're struggling with?

Ego says, *They're showing off.*

Reality? Their success is completely separate from yours, and there's no reason to compare—it doesn't take away from what you're capable of.

Ego distorts our ability to see things clearly. It replaces objectivity with self-centered interpretation, leading us to assume the worst in situations that might not even be about us.

Think about it—how many times have you overanalyzed a situation, replaying it in your mind, searching for hidden meanings that weren't even there? You convinced yourself that someone's mood, reaction, or decision was a reflection of you, when in reality, it had nothing to do with you at all. You created tension, felt resentment, or even withdrew—over something that only existed in *your* perception.

This is why unchecked ego can be so dangerous. It makes you reactive instead of rational. It turns neutral interactions into emotional landmines. It creates problems that don't actually exist and keeps you stuck in cycles of overthinking, self-doubt, and unnecessary conflict.

The truth is, most people are too consumed with their *own* lives, thoughts, and emotions to be constantly plotting against you. Most of the time, people are just acting based on their own priorities, struggles, and circumstances—*not* as a personal statement about you.

When you recognize that, you free yourself. You stop taking everything so personally. You stop making assumptions based on emotion. You learn to observe instead of react, to clarify instead of assume, and to move through life without the unnecessary weight of ego-driven stories.

Letting go of ego doesn't mean you don't value yourself—it means you understand that the world doesn't revolve around you. And that's a liberating realization.

How Ego Rewrites History to Fit Its Narrative

Ego is not just a bad storyteller—it's a straight-up liar.

It doesn't like facts. It likes *stories*—stories where you're always the one who was right, misunderstood, or treated unfairly. Ego doesn't care about objectivity or balance. It cares about *preserving your image*, even if that means distorting the truth.

Have you ever looked back on a situation and felt completely convinced you remembered it accurately—only to later realize you twisted the details to make yourself look better or someone else look worse?

That's ego manipulating your memory.

Ego downplays the things you did wrong and amplifies the things others did. It carefully edits the past, removing any inconvenient truths that might challenge your self-perception. It turns minor offenses into major betrayals, and it conveniently "forgets" the parts where *you* might have been in the wrong.

- You got into an argument with a friend? Ego remembers every insensitive thing *they* said but conveniently forgets the way *you* escalated it.
- You didn't get the recognition you wanted at work? Ego says your boss is unfair and overlooks how you might have missed key deadlines.

- You had a falling out with someone? Ego paints them as toxic while skipping over the moments when *you* could have handled things better.

Ego makes you believe your reactions were justified while everyone else was overreacting.

It makes you hold onto grudges long after the situation is over—because it convinces you that what happened was worse than it actually was. The more time passes, the more exaggerated the story becomes. Suddenly, a simple disagreement turns into *"They never respected me."* A minor slight turns into *"They were always out to get me."* And with each retelling, you become more of the victim and less of an active participant in the situation.

Ego loves rewriting history because it protects your identity. If admitting fault makes you feel weak, ego will twist the story until you never have to take responsibility. It tells you, *You didn't mess up—they did. You weren't wrong—you were wronged. You don't need to apologize—they do.*

But here's the truth: Reality doesn't care about your ego's version of events.

The past is what it is—whether you choose to face it honestly or not. And the longer you hold onto an ego-driven narrative, the longer you stay disconnected from the truth—and from the *growth* that comes with facing it.

Letting go of ego means being willing to look at yourself with honesty. It means admitting that sometimes, *you* were the one who misunderstood, overreacted, or made a mistake. It means realizing that rewriting history only keeps you stuck in the same patterns, while owning the truth allows you to move forward.

Your past doesn't define you, but your willingness to learn from it does.

How to Start Seeing Situations as They Are (Not as Your Ego Wants Them to Be)

So how do you break free from ego's distortions and start seeing reality clearly?

1. Ask Yourself: "Is This Really About Me?"

The next time you feel hurt, defensive, or offended, pause and ask yourself:

"Is this actually about me, or am I making it personal?"

99% of the time, it's *not* about you at all. People act based on their own thoughts, emotions, and experiences—not because of you. Their bad mood, their short response, their change in behavior—these things often have more to do with their own internal struggles than anything you did.

- Your friend canceled plans last minute? They might just be exhausted, not rejecting you.
- Your partner seemed distant today? They might be lost in thought, not losing interest.
- Your coworker didn't acknowledge your idea in the meeting? They might have been preoccupied, not dismissing you on purpose.

When you stop personalizing every situation, you *free yourself* from unnecessary suffering.

2. Challenge Your Version of the Story

Your ego wants to be the *main character*—the one who was right, justified, or wronged. But what if you're not seeing the whole picture?

Ask yourself:

- *"If I were in their shoes, how would I see this situation?"*
- *"If I removed my emotions from this, what's the actual truth?"*
- *"What part of this situation am I responsible for?"*

Ego loves to assign blame but resists accountability. It's easier to believe *they* were the problem than to admit you may have played a role. But reality isn't black and white. When you challenge your ego's version of events, you start to see a more *balanced* perspective.

- Maybe your friend *wasn't* ignoring you—they just had too much on their plate.
- Maybe your partner *wasn't* being insensitive—you just misinterpreted their words.
- Maybe your coworker *wasn't* trying to undermine you— they just had a different viewpoint.

The more you question your initial assumptions, the closer you get to reality.

3. Look at Facts, Not Feelings

Ego-driven thinking is *emotional thinking*. It makes you react based on *how something feels*, not what it actually is. But feelings aren't always facts.

Before jumping to conclusions, step back and look at the situation objectively:

- *Did they actually disrespect you, or did you just feel disrespected?*
- *Did they actually betray you, or did they just make a decision that wasn't about you?*
- *Did they actually mean harm, or are you assuming bad intentions?*

By focusing on *facts* instead of *feelings*, you strip away ego's filters and start seeing things as they truly are.

The truth is, ego thrives on illusion—but clarity comes from self-awareness. When you practice separating *what actually happened* from *what ego wants you to believe*, you become less reactive, less stressed, and more at peace with yourself and the world around you.

How Ego Turns You Into a Mind Reader (And Why You're Usually Wrong)

Let's be real—most of us are terrible at mind reading, but that doesn't stop ego from trying.

Ego doesn't like uncertainty. So when someone's behavior is unclear, ego fills in the blanks... and not in a good way.

Someone's quiet? "They're mad at me."

Someone's distant? "They must not care."

Someone doesn't text back? "I'm not important to them."

But here's the truth: **Most people aren't thinking about you as much as you think.**

They're wrapped up in their own lives, insecurities, fears, and distractions. And half the time, their behavior says more about their inner world than it ever says about you.

When ego tries to make you a mind reader, pause and remember:

- You don't know what's going on in someone else's world.
- You don't need to assign meaning to everything.
- It's okay to *not know*—that's where clarity begins.

Try this instead:

When you feel unsure, don't assume—ask.

When you feel rejected, don't spiral—breathe.

When you feel triggered, don't react—observe.

Most of your emotional suffering isn't from what actually happened.

It's from the story ego told you about what happened. And the more you question that story, the more peace you create.

Why You Shouldn't Judge People Through the Lens of Ego

When ego runs the show, you don't just misread situations—you misjudge people.

Ego wants fast conclusions. It wants certainty. It wants to define people quickly so it can feel in control.

But here's the truth: **you have no idea what someone has been through, what they're carrying, or who they're becoming.**

That's why judgment is one of ego's most dangerous habits.

Ego will:

- Judge someone's silence as arrogance—when really, they're just anxious.
- See someone's ambition as "too much"—when it's actually their way of surviving.
- Dismiss someone as "weird" or "different"—when that very difference might be their gift.

And when you judge people based on your ego's distorted view, you're not seeing *them*—you're seeing your *own projections.*

Think about high school.

The so-called "nerds" or quiet kids often got teased, misunderstood, or overlooked. But fast forward a few years—and they're the ones creating apps, leading companies, building careers, and changing the world.

Not because they needed to prove anything—but because they stayed focused on becoming who they were meant to be.

That's the power of growth.

And that's the danger of judging people too early, too harshly, or through the wrong lens.

Every single person is in a process.

What you see now is just a snapshot—not the full picture.

They are not their worst moment.

They are not their awkward phase.

They are not the label ego tried to give them.

You don't know where someone is going—and they might just surprise you.

Mini Mantra:

"The less I judge others, the more peace I create in myself."

Reflective Exercise: "Facts vs. Ego Filters"

This is a practical tool to help you separate what *actually happened* from what your *ego made it mean.*

Think of a recent situation that triggered you—maybe you felt offended, hurt, rejected, or overlooked.

Step 1: Describe the Situation (Just the Facts)

What actually happened?

Write only the *objective* facts. No feelings, no assumptions. Just the what, where, when, and how.

Step 2: What Did Your Ego Say?

What meaning did you attach to it?

Examples: "They don't respect me." "I'm being excluded." "I knew they didn't like me."

Step 3: What Else Could Be True?

Write at least 3 neutral or positive alternative explanations.

Challenge your ego's story. Ask: *What if this had nothing to do with me?*

Step 4: How Would Your Higher Self Respond?

From a place of clarity, how would you *choose* to see or respond now?

Bonus Prompt:

"When I stop assuming the worst, I give myself the best chance to grow."

Final Thoughts: The Power of Seeing Reality Clearly

Ego distorts. It personalizes. It rewrites.

But once you start questioning it, it loses its power over you.

- When you stop taking things personally, you stop feeling attacked.
- When you stop rewriting history, you start taking accountability.
- When you stop reacting based on ego's version of reality, you start responding based on truth.

And when you start seeing the world as it *really* is—not as your ego *wants* it to be—you finally start *living freely*.

Clarity is freedom. It means moving through life without the weight of imagined offenses, exaggerated betrayals, and false narratives. It means making decisions from a place of *awareness*, not from a place of emotional reactivity. It means understanding that not everything is about you, and not every feeling is a fact.

The journey to seeing reality clearly isn't about silencing your ego completely—it's about recognizing when it's speaking and choosing not to let it dictate your perception. The more you practice stepping outside of ego-driven thinking, the more you reclaim control over your mind, your emotions, and ultimately, your *life*.

The next chapter will dive into *how to rewire your mind to think beyond ego*—so you can stop living in illusion and start making choices from a place of true awareness.

Chapter 3: When Others Use Your Ego Against You

You already know ego can sabotage you from the inside—but what about when *other people* use your ego to sabotage you?

People are strategic. They learn what makes you tick. They figure out your weaknesses—even the ones you don't see in yourself. And if someone wants to keep you stuck, all they have to do is feed your ego in just the right way.

- **Some will hype you up when you're making terrible decisions—just to watch you fail.**
- **Some will manipulate you into thinking you're "winning" when you're actually losing.**
- **And some will put you down just enough to make sure you never grow past them.**

These people understand something most don't—*ego is predictable*. It craves validation and resists anything that challenges it. It's reactive, emotional, and easy to trigger. So, they use it like a puppet string—controlling your moves without you even realizing it.

- They stroke your ego when they want you blind to the truth.
- They challenge your ego when they want you distracted.
- They weaponize your need to "prove yourself" so you waste energy on the wrong things.

Think about it—how many times have you *insisted* on proving a point, just because someone made you feel like you had to? How many times have you doubled down on a bad decision just because admitting you were wrong would bruise your pride? How many times have you let yourself be led by *what feels good* rather than *what's actually good for you*?

That's how people trap you. They make you defend, chase, or prove something you *never had to* in the first place.

The sooner you recognize when people are using your ego against you, the sooner you stop falling for the trap. And once you stop being controlled by ego, you become *unshakable*.

How People Feed Your Ego for Your Downfall

Ego craves validation. It wants to feel *important*, *respected*, *admired*. And some people know this—so they give you exactly what you want, *just to set you up for failure.*

Think about it:

Have you ever had someone who only hypes you up when you're doing something reckless?

- That *friend* who loves when you start drama but is nowhere to be found when you need real support.
- That *coworker* who encourages you to quit your job on impulse, knowing you don't have a backup plan.
- That *person* who tells you your toxic habits are *"just part of who you are"* instead of helping you grow.

They *could* help you make better choices—but why would they, when they'd rather watch you crash and burn?

Frenemies Who Hype You Up When You're Making Bad Decisions

Some people love to see you fail—but they won't make it obvious. Instead of tearing you down, they *hype you up in the worst ways possible.*

- You're making impulsive, emotional decisions? *"Yesss, do it! Don't let anyone tell you what to do!"*
- You're about to make a major mistake? *"You don't need advice, trust your gut! You're unstoppable!"*
- You're ignoring red flags in a situation? *"That's just them hating on you. Keep doing what you're doing!"*

This is *not* real support. **This is manipulation.**

Real friends tell you the *truth*, even when you don't want to hear it.

Fake friends let you destroy yourself *while cheering you on.*

And the worst part? **Ego eats it up.**

Ego *loves* the idea that you're untouchable. That you don't need to listen to anyone. That you can do whatever you want without consequences. And people who want to see you fall *know this*. They don't challenge you because they *want* you to keep running full speed toward disaster.

They want you distracted.

They want you reactive.

44

They want you trapped in your own self-sabotage.

The question is: **Are you going to let them?**

How People Manipulate You Into Thinking You're Winning When You're Actually Losing

Some of the worst manipulators don't just let you make mistakes—they *trick* you into thinking you're winning when you're actually being played.

They use your ego against you, making you believe you're *in control* when, in reality, you're walking straight into a trap.

- **They make you chase the wrong goals.** Instead of focusing on *real* success, they get you obsessed with *status, drama, or empty victories.* You start prioritizing looking successful over actually *being* successful.

- **They convince you to compete with people who aren't even your competition.** Instead of growing, you waste time trying to "prove yourself" to people who *don't matter,* stuck in pointless rivalries while they sit back and watch.

- **They feed your need to be right—so you stop questioning yourself.** Instead of self-reflecting and improving, you double down on bad decisions, thinking your ego-driven confidence is actual wisdom.

Example: The Argument Trap

Imagine you're in a heated argument. You're emotional, reactive, and ready to prove a point. A real friend might say, *"Hey, take a breath. Think this through."*

But a manipulator? They'll say,

"You're totally right! Don't back down! Don't let them disrespect you!"

Ego *eats that up.* You feel *powerful, justified, unstoppable.*

But later?

You realize you *burned bridges, damaged relationships, and made a fool of yourself.*

You *"won"* the argument—but *at what cost?*

That's how people manipulate ego. They inflate your sense of importance just enough to make sure *you* are the one who self-destructs.

Because as long as you're focused on proving yourself, defending yourself, or chasing approval—

You're too distracted to actually win.

How People Put You Down So You Don't Surpass Them

Not everyone wants to see you win. Some people are perfectly happy *as long as you stay below them.*

And the easiest way to keep you stuck? **Plant doubt in your mind.**

- **They downplay your talents** so you never realize your full potential.

- **They criticize your ideas** so you don't have the confidence to take action.
- **They make you feel unqualified** so you never even *try*.

These people aren't always obvious. They don't openly tell you, *"I don't want you to succeed."* Instead, they operate *covertly*, planting seeds of uncertainty that slowly take root in your mind.

Example: The Subtle Doubt Tactic

You tell someone your big idea, excited and ready to take the next step. You expect encouragement, maybe even constructive feedback. Instead, you get:

- *"Are you sure you can pull that off?"*
- *"That sounds risky. What if it doesn't work?"*
- *"I mean, I don't know… seems kind of unrealistic."*

They don't actually **know** if your idea will work or not—but that's *not* the point. Their goal isn't logic. Their goal is to plant **just enough doubt** to make you second-guess yourself.

Because if you **succeed**?

- You might pass them.
- You might grow beyond what they expected.
- You might prove them wrong.

And that **terrifies** them.

Why Some People Can't Handle Your Growth

These aren't always enemies. Sometimes, they're people close to you—friends, family, even mentors. And often, they don't discourage you out of hate. They do it because **your success forces them to confront their own insecurities.**

- If you prove that *dreams can be achieved*, they lose their excuse for not chasing theirs.
- If you step outside the box, they have to question why they stayed inside it.
- If you grow, they have to ask themselves why they haven't.

It's easier for them to **hold you back** than to push themselves forward.

So instead of lifting you up, they subtly pull you down.

Not with outright insults.

Not with obvious sabotage.

But with **just enough discouragement** to keep you doubting yourself, hesitating, and staying *exactly where you are.*

The Truth: They're Scared of You Growing Past Them

The biggest reason people try to manipulate or undermine you? **They're scared.**

Not always consciously. Some people don't even realize why they act the way they do. But deep down, fear drives their actions:

- **They're scared you'll outgrow them.** If you rise above them, they'll lose the comfort of being "better" than you.

- **They're scared your success will expose their lack of progress.** Watching you chase your dreams reminds them of everything they *haven't* done.
- **They're scared that if you level up, they'll have to level up too.** And they're *not* ready for that responsibility.

So instead of supporting your growth, **they try to control your ego**—because controlling your ego means controlling *you*.

The Three Ways People Control Your Ego
They Hype You Up When You're Making Mistakes
- They don't want you to get better, so they make bad decisions feel like good ones.
- They'll say, *"You don't need to change, you're perfect as you are!"*—even when your habits are holding you back.
- They'll encourage reckless behavior, feeding your impulsiveness so you never pause to reflect.

They Manipulate Your Perception of Success
- They push you toward *flashy* but empty goals—status, drama, attention—so you waste time chasing illusions instead of real progress.
- They make you compete with people who aren't even your competition, keeping you distracted.
- They tell you you're already "winning" to keep you from striving for *real* success.

They Put You Down Just Enough to Keep You from Believing in Yourself

- They subtly undermine your confidence, planting doubt so you never fully commit to your goals.
- They phrase their discouragement as "concern":
- *"I just don't want you to get your hopes up."*
- *"Are you sure you can handle that?"*
- *"Most people fail at that—it's really hard."*
- They don't want you to quit, but they don't want you to *succeed too much*, either.

Breaking Free: How to Stop Falling for the Trap

The key to escaping this cycle? **See the game and stop playing it.**

Every time someone tries to control your ego, **pause and question it.**

When someone hypes you up, ask yourself:

- *"Are they actually supporting me, or are they just encouraging my worst habits?"*
- *"Is this real confidence, or just an ego boost?"*

When someone criticizes you, ask yourself:

- *"Is this valid feedback, or are they just projecting their own fears onto me?"*
- *"Would they say this to someone they truly believed in?"*

When someone makes you feel unqualified, ask yourself:

- *"Do I actually lack skills, or are they just afraid of what I could become?"*
- *"Am I doubting myself because of facts, or because of their opinion?"*

The truth is, **your success will make some people uncomfortable.**

And that's *okay*. Because the ones who truly support you? **They won't try to manipulate your ego.** They'll challenge you in ways that help you grow. They'll push you toward *real* confidence, not just shallow validation.

The moment you recognize these tactics, they stop working on you.

And once you take your ego out of the equation, **you stop making emotional, reactive decisions—and start making choices based on truth.**

That's when you become *truly unstoppable.*

The Weaponization of Praise

Not all praise is helpful—**some of it is a trap**.

People always talk about how damaging criticism can be, but the truth is, flattery can be just as dangerous—**especially when it's aimed at your ego, not your growth.**

Sometimes people don't manipulate you by tearing you down. They do it by lifting you up *just enough* to keep you blind.

They'll say things like:

"You're so much better than them, why should you even listen?"

"You always know what to do—you don't need anyone's advice."

"You're untouchable—nothing can stop you."

And at first? It feels good. It feels validating. It feels like support.

But here's what it *really* does:

- **It blinds you to your blind spots.**

  You stop questioning yourself, even when you should.

- **It pushes you into arrogance.**

  You start thinking you're above feedback, correction, or reflection.

- **It isolates you from growth.**

  You ignore people who are actually trying to help you improve, because now you're surrounded by "yes-men" who only say what your ego wants to hear.

This is how ego gets used as a leash.

You think you're running free, but you're actually being led—in the exact direction they want you to go.

They don't need to control you directly. All they have to do is feed your pride and let your ego do the rest.

Because when you're operating from that inflated sense of self, you're no longer checking your blind spots, listening to wise counsel, or making decisions rooted in truth.

You're acting from hype—not discernment.

And that's exactly how you get played.

Reminder:

Real confidence isn't afraid of correction.

Real confidence listens, reflects, adjusts.

Real friends want to see you elevate—even if that means challenging you, disagreeing with you, or holding up a mirror when you're off track.

They don't feed your ego just to stay on your good side. They call you higher—even when it's uncomfortable.

Because true support doesn't always feel good in the moment. But it always leaves you better in the end.

Reflective Exercise: Who's Pulling the Strings?

This is about checking your emotional reactions and recognizing patterns where your ego has been influenced by someone else.

Step 1: Identify the Moment Think of a recent time when you...

- Felt the need to prove yourself
- Made a decision that felt impulsive or reactive
- Doubted yourself after someone's comment

Step 2: Ask These Questions

1. *Was I acting from confidence or ego?*
2. *Did someone hype me up in a way that encouraged recklessness instead of growth?*
3. *Did someone plant a seed of doubt that made me question my worth or ability?*

4. *Did I make that choice because I truly believed in it—or because I didn't want to look weak or wrong?*

Step 3: Reclaim Your Power Write out one thing you would have done differently if you were acting from your highest self instead of ego.

Then finish this prompt:

"Next time someone tries to trigger my ego, I will respond by..."

Final Thoughts: Reclaiming Control Over Your Ego

Ego is powerful, but it's also **easily controlled**—by *you* or by *other people.*

If you don't learn how to **master it**, someone else *will.*

People will use your ego to push you in the direction *they* want—whether that means hyping you up into making reckless choices or tearing you down just enough to make you hesitate.

So the next time someone:

- Overly hypes you up
- Subtly plants doubt in your mind
- Tries to manipulate your confidence

Pause. Think. Ask yourself what their real intentions are.

- *Are they genuinely supporting me, or are they feeding my ego to control my actions?*
- *Is this criticism valid, or is it meant to keep me small?*
- *Am I reacting from a place of confidence or a place of insecurity?*

Because the people who **truly** want to see you win? They won't play games with your ego.

And the ones who **do**?

They were *never* in your corner to begin with.

Reclaiming control over your ego means **freeing yourself**—from manipulation, from self-sabotage, and from the invisible strings people try to pull.

The next chapter will show you how to build **true confidence**—the kind that doesn't rely on ego, but on *real* self-awareness and self-mastery. Because when you know who you are, **no one can use your ego against you.**

Chapter 4: Escaping the Self-Sabotage Cycle

Ego is a master of self-sabotage—but the worst part? **Most people don't even realize when they're doing it.**

It's easy to point fingers and say, *"That person's ego is out of control."* But when it comes to ourselves? Ego convinces us that:

- *We're justified.*
- *We're right.*
- *We're not the problem.*

Ego doesn't announce itself. It disguises self-sabotage as **self-protection, confidence, or even strength.**

- **You burn bridges** and call it *standing your ground.*
- **You reject feedback** and call it *trusting yourself.*
- **You push away opportunities** and call it *not settling.*

And the more you let ego run the show, the harder it is to see when **you're the one getting in your own way.**

That's why breaking the cycle of self-sabotage **isn't about fighting your ego**—because ego *loves* resistance. Instead, it's about **recognizing when ego is working against you** and taking control *before it does any damage.*

Because the truth is—**ego isn't your enemy.** But when you don't know how to manage it, it can **become one.**

How to Recognize When Your Ego is Working Against You

If you want to break free from **ego-driven self-sabotage**, the first step is to **catch it in action.**

Ego doesn't always scream—it whispers. It disguises itself as confidence, self-protection, and even logic. But when you look closer, you'll see it for what it really is: **fear in disguise.**

Here's how you know **your ego is controlling you:**

You take everything personally.
- A simple comment, a piece of feedback, or even someone else's success feels like a personal attack.
- You assume people's actions are always about *you*, even when they have nothing to do with you.

You get defensive instead of listening.
- Instead of seeking to understand, you **shut down or argue** just to "win" the conversation.
- You take disagreement as disrespect rather than seeing it as a different perspective.

You reject criticism—even when it's valid.
- Because admitting fault **feels like losing.**
- You'd rather justify a mistake than learn from it.

You make decisions based on proving yourself.
- Instead of doing what's **best** for you, you focus on what *looks* successful.

- You chase validation rather than real progress.

You stay in unhealthy situations out of pride.
- Whether it's a **relationship, job, or friendship**, you refuse to leave because you don't want to "lose."
- You convince yourself it's "not that bad" just to avoid admitting you made a mistake.

Ego thrives in these moments. It makes you feel powerful while **secretly keeping you stuck.**

But the moment you recognize these patterns?

You can start breaking free.

How to Listen Without Reacting—Mastering Self-Awareness

One of the biggest signs of an **ego-driven mind? Reacting instead of responding.**

Ego makes you **impulsive.** It makes you **take things personally.** It distorts what you hear, making you focus more on how something makes you *feel* rather than what's actually being said.

When your ego is in control, you listen through a **filter of emotion**—not logic. You hear **criticism as an attack, advice as judgment,** and **someone else's success as a personal challenge.** Instead of taking in the message, you prepare a defense, cut people off, or shut down completely.

But true self-awareness isn't about reacting—it's about recognizing your triggers and **choosing how to respond.**

So how do you break the habit?

1. Create Space Between Stimulus and Reaction

When something **triggers** you, your ego wants you to **react immediately.** To prove a point. To defend yourself. To "win."

But winning a reactionary battle often means *losing in the bigger picture.*

The **solution? Pause.**

Before you respond, take a deep breath. Even a few seconds of space can stop you from making an **ego-driven** decision that you'll regret later.

Then, ask yourself:

- **Am I reacting out of emotion or logic?**
- **Am I feeling attacked, or is this just my ego talking?**
- **Is this something I actually need to defend, or is my pride making me defensive?**
- **What is the actual message here, beyond how I feel about it?**

This small moment of self-awareness **interrupts the cycle** of automatic emotional responses.

It gives you **control** over how you respond, instead of letting your ego dictate the conversation.

And when you respond with **clarity** instead of ego, you communicate better, avoid unnecessary conflicts, and keep yourself from being **manipulated** by emotional triggers.

2. Listen to Understand, Not to Respond

Most people don't actually listen.

They **wait for their turn to talk.**

They **scan for weaknesses in what's being said.**

They **prepare a defense instead of absorbing the message.**

And that's exactly what ego wants.

But true listening—the kind that leads to **growth, understanding, and stronger relationships**—is about taking in **the full message** before reacting.

Try this instead:

- Instead of **waiting for your turn to talk,** focus entirely on what's being said.
- Instead of **looking for flaws,** see if there's any truth in it—even if it's uncomfortable.
- Instead of **getting defensive,** ask yourself, *"What can I learn from this?"*

Because here's the truth: **Not everything that challenges you is an attack.**

- A friend giving you feedback doesn't mean they don't support you.
- Someone disagreeing with you doesn't mean they're against you.
- Someone else succeeding doesn't mean you're failing.

When your ego controls how you listen, you **twist the meaning** of what's being said. But when you remove ego, you see things **as they truly are.**

3. Recognize When Your Ego is Trying to "Win" Instead of Grow

Ego wants you to be **right** more than it wants you to be **better.**

That's why so many people get stuck in arguments, repeating the same points over and over—because they're more focused on **winning** than actually understanding.

But ask yourself:

- **Do I want to be right, or do I want to learn?**
- **Am I holding onto my perspective because it's actually right, or because I don't want to admit I was wrong?**
- **Is this argument serving me, or just feeding my ego?**
- The goal isn't to "win" every conversation—it's to **grow from it.**

4. Detach Emotion From The Message

Sometimes, even when something is **true**, it stings.

- Maybe someone points out a flaw you don't want to admit.
- Maybe someone challenges your opinion, and you feel exposed.
- Maybe someone gives you advice, and your first instinct is to **reject it** out of pride.

But truth doesn't care about **how it makes you feel.** It exists whether you accept it or not.

So when you hear something uncomfortable, **pause before reacting emotionally.**

Ask yourself:

- **Does this message hold truth, even if it's uncomfortable?**

- Is my ego resisting this because I don't want to face it?
- If I set aside my pride, would this actually help me grow?

The moment you stop reacting *emotionally* and start listening *objectively*, you gain **control over your mind.**

5. Practice the Art of Neutrality

The most powerful mindset shift? **Not everything needs a reaction.**

Some things are better left **unbothered.** Some people are better left **unengaged.** Some battles are better left **unfought.**

Ego tells you to **respond to everything.** To defend, explain, argue, or react. But true self-awareness means knowing **when to stay silent, when to walk away, and when to let things be.**

So the next time you feel yourself getting **triggered, defensive, or emotional—**

Pause.

Take a breath.

Choose to **listen, reflect, and respond with intention.**

Because when you stop **reacting** and start **listening,** ego loses its grip on you.

And when ego loses control, you gain **clarity, confidence, and real self-awareness.**

How to Turn Criticism into Growth Instead of an Ego Trigger

Criticism is one of **ego's biggest weaknesses.**

It hates being told it's wrong.

It hates being questioned.

It hates feeling like it's not good enough.

But here's the truth: **Criticism is one of the most valuable tools for growth—if you know how to handle it.**

Ego wants you to take criticism **personally.** It wants you to see it as an **attack** instead of an **opportunity to improve.** But the most successful people in the world **don't avoid criticism**—they *use* it. They **turn feedback into fuel** instead of letting it break them down.

So how do you shift from **ego-driven reactions** to **growth-focused thinking?**

Step 1: Reframe the Way You See Criticism

Your **initial reaction** to criticism is often ego-driven. But you can **rewire your response** by changing how you interpret it.

Instead of seeing criticism as a **threat**, see it as **insight.**

Mindset Shifts:

Old mindset: *"They're attacking me."*

New mindset: *"They're offering a perspective I might not see."*

Old mindset: *"They don't know what they're talking about."*

New mindset: *"Let me consider if there's something to learn here."*

Old mindset: *"I have to prove them wrong."*

New mindset: *"I don't have to prove anything. I just have to improve."*

The moment you stop seeing criticism as an attack, you take away ego's power.

63

Step 2: Separate Emotion from Information

Not all criticism is **valid**, but almost all criticism can **teach you something.** The key is to **filter the message from the emotions attached to it.**

Ask yourself:

- *Is this person trying to help me or just hurt me?*
- *Even if their delivery was harsh, is there truth in what they're saying?*
- *If I strip away my emotions, does this feedback give me something to improve?*

Criticism **stings** when you let it attack your **identity.** But when you see it as information instead of an insult, it becomes **useful instead of painful.**

Example:

Someone tells you, *"You never listen to feedback."* Your ego's reaction: *"That's not true! They're just being negative."* A growth-based response: *"Let me reflect—are there times I've dismissed feedback too quickly?"*

Once you learn to **separate emotion from feedback**, you stop reacting **defensively** and start improving **intentionally.**

Step 3: Know When to Ignore and When to Absorb

Not all criticism deserves your energy. Some people just want to bring you down. **The key is knowing the difference.**

- **If the criticism is constructive** → *Listen and learn.*
- **If the criticism is destructive** → *Ignore and move on.*

Signs of constructive criticism:

It's specific (*"Here's something you can improve on..."*)

It comes from someone with experience or insight

It's meant to help, not just hurt

Signs of destructive criticism:

It's vague (*"You suck" or "That's stupid"*)

It's coming from someone who isn't adding value

It's meant to tear you down, not lift you up

Not all feedback is **worth absorbing**—but the ability to take in the **right** criticism is what separates people who **grow** from people who **stay stuck.**

Step 4: Apply It and Move Forward

Growth happens when you take criticism and **do something with it.**

- **Listen.** Don't dismiss feedback just because it stings.
- **Filter.** Take what's useful, ignore what's not.
- **Apply.** Make adjustments where needed.

When you use criticism to **elevate yourself,** ego loses its grip. You stop **taking things personally** and start **using everything as a tool to level up.**

Signs Your Ego is Healing

The goal **isn't** to destroy your ego—it's to **master it.** To make it **work for you** instead of against you.

Ego isn't the enemy. It's a tool. And when you learn how to **control it instead of letting it control you**, you start moving through life with **clarity, confidence, and purpose.**

Here's how you know **your ego is healing:**

You stop taking everything personally.
- You realize that **most things aren't about you.**
- Other people's **opinions, actions, and decisions** are based on **them—not you.**
- You no longer waste energy **overanalyzing** why someone did or didn't do something.

Example:
Before: *"They didn't invite me. They must not like me."*
After: *"Maybe they had their reasons. It's not about me."*

The more you **detach your self-worth from external situations**, the freer you become.

You learn from mistakes instead of defending them.
- You stop making **excuses** and start making **improvements.**
- Instead of **avoiding accountability**, you **own your mistakes**—and grow from them.
- You see mistakes as **lessons**, not **threats to your identity.**

Example:
Before: *"I didn't mess up! That's just how I am."*

After: *"I could've handled that better. What can I do differently next time?"*

The moment you stop **defending your flaws**, you create space to **fix them.**

You focus on growth instead of proving yourself.
- Instead of needing to **be right**, you focus on **getting better.**
- Instead of seeking **validation**, you seek **wisdom.**
- Instead of defending your **old self**, you focus on **evolving into your best self.**

Example:
Before: *"I have to prove I'm the best."*
After: *"I have to keep learning and improving."*

Growth is **endless.** And when your ego stops obsessing over **proving your worth**, you free yourself to **actually become your best.**

A **healed ego** doesn't need to be fed. It doesn't crave **constant validation, endless competition, or external approval.**

A **healed ego** is **secure enough to grow, learn, and evolve—without fear.**

The Mirror vs. The Mask

Ego doesn't just sabotage you in obvious ways—it plays a quiet, clever trick.

It doesn't destroy your growth.

It *disguises* it.

It replaces your mirror with a mask.

The Mirror: Truth, Reflection, and Growth

A mirror shows you everything as it is—not as you wish it were.
It reflects the full picture:

- Your strengths and talents.
- Your flaws and blind spots.
- The patterns you keep repeating.
- The habits that help you, and the ones that don't.

Looking into the mirror of self-awareness is uncomfortable.
It asks you to be honest about how you show up.
It asks you to own your part in your struggles.
It asks you to reflect, adjust, and evolve.

But it also gives you the truth you need to change your life.
Because **you can't fix what you won't face.**
And without the mirror, you're just guessing your way through self-improvement.

The mirror doesn't judge—it reveals.
And that's exactly why it's powerful.

The Mask: Image, Illusion, and Ego-Protection

Now the mask?
The mask tells a different story.
The mask shows who you *want* to be seen as—not who you actually are.
It says:

- "I've got it all together."
- "I don't need help."
- "I'm not wrong. I'm just misunderstood."
- "I'm confident" — when really, you're scared of being exposed.

The mask hides the insecurities. The fears. The vulnerability. But here's the problem:

When you live behind a mask, even the praise you get doesn't feel real—because it's not for the real you.

You're not just fooling others—you're slowly fooling yourself.
You start to believe the performance.
You stop looking in the mirror altogether.
And before you know it, you've built a life around protecting an identity instead of becoming your fullest self.

The Cost of Choosing the Mask

Every time you choose the mask over the mirror, you trade progress for protection.

- You avoid growth to protect your image.
- You reject feedback to avoid discomfort.
- You pretend to be okay instead of asking for what you need.
- You make ego-driven decisions that look good but don't feel good.

And the longer you wear the mask, the heavier it gets.
It starts to feel suffocating.

Because deep down, you *know* there's more to you than the version you've been performing.

The Reframe

"Am I wearing a mask to protect my ego... or facing the mirror to grow?"

Because the truth is:

Growth doesn't require perfection. It requires **honesty.** It requires the courage to say:

- "This habit isn't serving me."
- "I overreacted, and I want to do better."
- "I don't have all the answers, but I'm willing to learn."

Every time you choose the mirror, you choose **freedom.**
You stop performing, and you start evolving.
You stop defending yourself, and you start discovering yourself.

And once you take off the mask and face your reflection with love and truth?

That's when you unlock the version of you that can't be stopped.

Reflective Exercise: Spot the Sabotage

This is all about identifying where ego has been running your life in the background—and helping you stop the cycle before it repeats.

Step 1: Identify a Recent Self-Sabotage Pattern

Think of a recent moment where something didn't go as planned.

It could be a:

- Conflict you escalated
- Feedback you rejected
- Opportunity you missed
- Relationship you distanced yourself from

Then, answer:

1. What happened? (Describe the situation briefly.)

2. What was my initial emotional reaction?

3. Did I act out of ego? (Examples: defensiveness, pride, proving a point, avoiding vulnerability)

4. What was I protecting—my growth or my image?

5. What would I do differently now, knowing what I know about ego?

Step 2: Make It Practical

Complete this sentence:

"The next time I feel the urge to defend, prove, or justify—I'll pause and ask myself:

Is this helping me grow or just helping my ego feel safe?"

Write that somewhere you'll see it. Sticky note. Journal. Lock screen.

Because awareness is what breaks the cycle.

Final Thoughts: Mastering Your Ego, Mastering Your Life

Ego is a tricky thing. It can **build you up**, but it can also **tear you down.** It can make you feel **powerful** while secretly keeping you **trapped in weakness.**

But once you **recognize how it works? It loses control over you.**

- When you **stop reacting** and start **responding**, you gain **clarity.**
- When you **stop taking things personally**, you gain **peace.**
- When you **stop proving yourself** and start **improving yourself**, you gain **true power.**

You don't have to destroy your ego—you just have to **master it.**

The next chapter will take things even further—**teaching you how to turn ego from an enemy into an ally.** Because when you **master your ego**, you **master everything.**

Chapter 5: The Mask of "I Don't Care" – Ego's Favorite Lie

You ever notice how people say "I don't care" the *most* when they clearly do?

Yeah... that's not strength — that's ego in full disguise.

Saying you don't care has become a reflex. It's like a built-in auto-reply that keeps you from admitting you're hurt, disappointed, scared, or *way too invested*. But here's the truth: "I don't care" is rarely honest. It's not peace — it's avoidance. It's a mask the ego throws on when vulnerability feels too risky.

Because let's face it — caring means you're open. And when you're open, people can *hurt* you. So instead of saying, "That actually bothered me," we armor up with apathy. We act unbothered, unfazed, above it all. But deep down? You feel everything. You just don't want anyone to know.

The Illusion of Control

The ego loves pretending it's in control — and apathy *looks* like control. When you act like nothing gets to you, you feel powerful. Like you've mastered detachment. Like you're above the drama. You might even convince yourself you're emotionally evolved. But let's call it what it really is: performance.

You're not in control — you're just emotionally avoiding the parts of life that make you feel vulnerable. Apathy becomes a convenient mask, because caring makes you feel exposed. And to the ego, vulnerability equals weakness. So it tells you: *"Let it go. Don't react. You're better than that. You don't care."*

But deep down? You do.

The problem is, pretending not to care doesn't protect you — it *disconnects* you. From others. From joy. From truth. And worst of all... from *yourself.*

It numbs the pain, sure — but it also numbs the possibility of healing. You think you're rising above, but you're really just pressing pause on your own growth. The ego doesn't want you to feel — because if you feel, you *might* have to change. And change requires humility.

That "I don't care" attitude? It's a survival strategy — but it's also self-sabotage. It shields you from pain in the short term, but it builds emotional walls so high that nothing real can get through. Love can't. Peace can't. Fulfillment can't. You're not detached — you're *stuck.*

It's like emotional constipation: you're holding so much in that nothing can move. You're full of words you didn't say, tears you didn't cry, and truths you didn't admit to yourself. That's not power — that's pressure.

True control comes from *facing* your emotions, not burying them.
From choosing how you respond, not pretending you don't feel.
From staying soft in a hard world — and still standing tall.

Apathy Isn't Power — Honesty Is

Here's the truth bomb:

There   is   nothing   weak   about   feeling   things.
There is nothing foolish about caring, loving deeply, or wanting more from life or from people.

74

Somewhere along the way, we were taught that emotions make us fragile. That expressing how we feel is "too much," or that caring too openly makes us look desperate, clingy, dramatic, or soft. But you know what's actually soft? Letting your ego punk you into silence.

You know what's powerful? Emotional honesty. The kind that says, "Yeah, I felt that. I'm human. But I'm still standing."

You can say:

- "That hurt me, but I'm not going to let it define me."
- "I care about this, and that's okay."
- "I'm disappointed, but I'm still proud of how I showed up."
- "That didn't turn out how I hoped, but I'm not ashamed for hoping."

That's not weakness. That's *mastery*. That's you choosing to be self-aware rather than self-denying.

Because pretending not to care? That's performative. But owning your truth with grace and composure? That's power.

Apathy is a wall. Honesty is a mirror. One keeps people out. The other lets you see yourself clearly.

And look — honesty doesn't mean being messy or emotionally explosive. It doesn't mean over-sharing or spilling your heart to people who don't deserve access. It means *you're in alignment* with yourself. It means you know what's going on inside you — and you're not ashamed of it.

Because being emotionally honest doesn't mean your emotions run you. It means they don't *control you from the shadows*. You've brought them into the light. You've named them. And once something has a name, it can be processed, handled, and healed.

That's real strength.

That's emotional intelligence.

That's ego in check — *not in charge.*

How to Be Emotionally Honest Without Losing Your Power

Here's the thing: letting your guard down doesn't mean you're weak.

Being vulnerable doesn't mean you're messy, dramatic, or "doing too much."

It means you're in touch with yourself. And that's a flex.

You can be open and still have boundaries.

You can express yourself *and* protect your peace.

You can care deeply *without being controlled* by how people respond to that care.

The goal isn't to harden up — it's to soften *without breaking.* It's to stop leaking power through suppression and start standing in power through honesty.

Here's how to do both:

Name your emotion, don't judge it.

The first step to emotional honesty is *awareness.* You have to know what you're feeling — and stop punishing yourself for feeling it.

Instead of pushing emotions down or labeling them as "bad" or "weak," just name them:

- "I feel hurt."
- "I feel excited but nervous."
- "I feel overlooked."
- "I feel vulnerable right now."

That's it. No overthinking, no shame spiral. Just truth. Emotions aren't permanent — they're messengers. When you acknowledge them, they move. When you avoid them, they stay trapped.

Let it pass *through* you — don't let it control you from behind the scenes.

Speak from your truth, not your ego.

Ego wants the last word. Truth wants to be heard.

When someone disappoints you, ego says:

"Whatever. I'm good. I don't care."

But truth says:

"That impacted me. I'm still processing it. I care, and I'm figuring out what that means for me."

Your truth is never too much. What's "too much" is the energy it takes to keep lying to yourself just to appear strong. Say what's real — not what sounds cool.

Speaking from your truth doesn't mean oversharing. It means you're grounded in your feelings and intentional with your words. You're not reacting — you're responding.

Set boundaries, not walls.

There's a difference between self-respect and emotional isolation. Boundaries are built from clarity and love. Walls are built from fear and protection.

- Boundaries say: "This is where I end and you begin."
- Walls say: "No one gets in — ever."

You don't need to become emotionally cold to stay safe. You just need to be clear about what you allow, what you tolerate, and what you're no longer available for.

Boundaries are loving — they protect your peace without locking you in a cage of apathy.

Care consciously.

Let's be real: you're *always* going to care. Even when you say you don't. So instead of pretending not to care, be intentional about *what* and *who* gets your energy.

- Is this worth your emotional investment?
- Is this someone who honors your care?
- Is this situation in alignment with your values?

Protecting your peace doesn't mean going numb. It means *choosing* your focus. It means showing up for what matters — and releasing what doesn't without bitterness.

You don't have to stop caring. You just have to stop caring about things that drain you.

Emotional honesty is not the enemy of power — it's the foundation of it.

Power without truth is just ego in costume.

The real flex? Feeling everything, owning it, and still walking forward with your head high.

The Mask of "I Don't Care" – Ego's Favorite Lie
The Social Mask We Learn to Wear

A big reason "I don't care" becomes so reflexive is because we're taught from a young age that *not caring* equals power. Think about it:

- In school, the cool kids didn't care.
- In relationships, the one who "cares less" is seen as the one with the upper hand.
- In arguments, the one who walks away unbothered is seen as the one who "won."

So what do we learn? That the safest way to protect ourselves is to care *less* — or at least act like it.

But that creates a major internal split: You *do* care — deeply — but you don't feel safe showing it. So the ego steps in with the performance. The *mask*.

But here's the problem:

When you constantly pretend not to care, you lose connection with the part of you that actually does — and that's the part that fuels joy, growth, empathy, and purpose.

The truth is: **you were never meant to be indifferent.** You were meant to be resilient *and* emotionally alive. You can have emotional boundaries *without* emotional detachment.

Why the "I Don't Care" Mask Is So Addictive

The mask becomes a coping mechanism — one that *feels* like freedom but actually traps you in disconnection.

- It protects your ego from rejection.
- It numbs uncomfortable truths.
- It keeps you "safe" from vulnerability — but at the cost of real connection.

And like any mask, it starts to feel normal. Comfortable. Even necessary.

But the more you wear it, the more you forget what your real face even looks like.

Letting the Mask Go: Reconnecting with the Part of You That Cares

So how do you take the mask off *without* falling apart?

You start by acknowledging this:

You're allowed to care.

You're allowed to be disappointed.

You're allowed to want more, expect better, and feel let down when people or life fall short.

And you're still powerful when you do.

Caring doesn't make you weak.

It means you're paying attention. It means you're invested. It means you're human.

And when you learn to care *without attachment, without ego, without trying to control the outcome* — that's emotional mastery.

When Apathy Becomes a Lifestyle — And You Lose Your Inner Child

Here's something that doesn't get talked about enough:

The more you say "I don't care," the more you actually stop caring.

Not just about the things that hurt — but about the things that used to light you up.

What starts as a defense mechanism eventually becomes a personality trait. Apathy turns from something you *say* to something you *become*. And that's when the real danger sets in.

You stop feeling excited.

You stop dreaming big.

You stop letting yourself hope, because hope feels like a setup. You tell yourself you're "mature" now, "realistic," "grown." But really?

You just disconnected from your inner child — the part of you that used to:

- Get curious instead of jaded
- Love freely without fear of being "too much"
- Believe in second chances and magical outcomes
- Cry when something mattered and laugh with your whole body when it didn't

That part of you didn't die — it got buried under the weight of pretending not to care.

And the longer you live like that, the harder it is to access that softness again. The dreamer. The lover. The feeler. The believer.

But here's the truth:

Growing up isn't about feeling *less* — it's about learning how to feel fully **without letting those feelings control you.** Maturity isn't numbness — it's emotional regulation.

The strongest people aren't cold. They're the ones who can feel *everything* without shutting down. And the ones who grow the most? They never lose touch with the part of themselves that still cares deeply — even when it's hard.

Reflective Exercise: What's Beneath Your "I Don't Care"?

Grab a notebook, or just sit with yourself for a few minutes. No distractions. No filters. **Just honesty.**

Answer these prompts without overthinking:

1. What's something (or someone) I recently told myself I "don't care" about?

   (Be honest. It can be a small moment or something big that stung more than you'd like to admit.)

2. Why did I say I didn't care?

3. Was I trying to protect myself?

4. Did I feel out of control?

5. Was I scared to be disappointed again?

6. What emotion was I *really* feeling beneath the apathy?

   (Examples: hurt, jealousy, rejection, sadness, fear, embarrassment.)

7. What would I have said or done if I gave myself permission to *actually feel* that emotion?

   (*How would I have shown up if I didn't let my ego speak for me?*)

8. How can I respond differently next time — with honesty and strength, not ego and numbness?

9. What would it mean about me if I admitted I cared?

   (*Does it make me feel needy? Soft? Dependent? Why?*)

10. What part of myself am I trying to protect when I say "I don't care"?

11. Where did I first learn that caring was dangerous, embarrassing, or "too much"?

12. Who am I trying to convince — others, or myself?

13. What would happen if I was honest about what I feel, even if it was just with myself?

Reminder: You don't have to pretend to be cold to be strong. Real ones feel deeply and still rise.

Final Thoughts

If "I don't care" is your go-to line, ask yourself: *What am I trying to avoid?*

Most times, it's the discomfort of being seen in your rawest form. But that rawness? That's where your power is.

Ego wants you to stay numb. But you weren't born to be cold — you were born to be real.

Part 2: The Modern-Day Ego Trap

How Society Fuels the Problem

It's not just you. The world you live in is designed to feed your ego—and starve your soul.

We're constantly bombarded with messages telling us we're not enough. Social media, advertising, fake perfection, hustle culture, status games—it's all ego food. And the more you consume it, the more disconnected you become from who you *actually* are.

Society teaches you to look outward for your worth: how you look, what you have, who validates you, how successful you appear. But none of that truly fills you. It just keeps your ego in the driver's seat, chasing external wins while your inner world falls apart.

This part of the book is about waking up from that matrix. We're calling out the systems, the trends, and the subtle conditioning that tricks you into thinking ego is confidence, when really—it's insecurity dressed up as self-worth.

You're not crazy for feeling lost in all of it.

You're just waking up.

And once you do, the game changes.

Chapter 6: How Social Media Traps You in Ego

Social media is one of the **biggest ego traps** of modern life. It's designed to make you **obsessed with validation, perception, and approval.**

- **Every like** gives your brain a **dopamine hit.**
- **Every comment** feels like **confirmation of your worth.**
- **Every follower** makes you feel **more important.**

It feels powerful.

It feels like connection.

But in reality? **It's an illusion.**

Social media doesn't actually **build** self-worth—it creates **dependency** on external validation. And when **ego** starts chasing that validation, you fall into a cycle that's **hard to break.**

You start measuring your **value** by:

- How many people **approve of you.**
- How many **views, likes, and shares** you get.
- How you compare to **everyone else online.**

And the worst part? **It never feels like enough.**

Even when you reach one level of validation, **ego craves more.** More attention. More recognition. More approval.

The result?

- You start shaping your **identity** around what gets the most **engagement** instead of what's real.

- You start prioritizing **how things look** over how they **actually feel.**
- You start **seeking attention** instead of **seeking truth.**

And before you know it, **social media isn't just something you use—it's something that controls you.**

The Addiction to Validation—Why Likes, Comments, and Attention Feel So Powerful

Social media is like a **slot machine for your ego.**

Every time you post, you subconsciously ask:

- *Will people approve of this?*
- *Will I get attention for this?*
- *Will this make me look successful, attractive, or interesting?*

And when the likes, comments, and shares roll in, **your brain rewards you.**

Ding! A like = *approval.*

Ding! A comment = *validation.*

Ding! A share = *importance.*

Each notification gives you a **small dopamine rush**—the same chemical that fuels **gambling addiction.**

And just like with gambling, the more you **chase it,** the harder it is to **stop.**

The Real Danger?

It's not just about the **dopamine hits**—it's about what happens when social media starts controlling how you **see yourself.**

When you start equating attention with worth.

- If a post **does well,** you feel *valuable, interesting, and important.*
- If it **flops,** you feel *ignored, invisible, or not good enough.*

When you feel less valuable if a post doesn't do well.

- You start believing your **value fluctuates** based on how many people engage with you online.

When you need constant validation to feel good about yourself.

- You become **dependent on external approval**, unable to feel confident unless others confirm it.

How Ego Gets Trapped in the Validation Cycle

Ego **thrives** in this environment. It makes you:

Crave approval.

Fear being ignored.

Make choices based on how they look, not how they feel.

Instead of asking: *"What do I actually want?"*

You start asking: *"What will get the most attention?"*

Instead of living for **yourself**, you start performing for **others.**

And that's how social media **traps you.** Not by forcing you—but by making you **feel like you need it.**

How Online Personas Fuel Ego-Driven Identity

Social media doesn't just **amplify** ego—it creates entire **false identities.**

Think about it:

- People only post **the best moments**, never the struggles.
- They filter their lives to appear **happier, richer, more successful.**
- They **curate their personalities** to fit whatever gets the most engagement.

And after a while, **even they start believing their own illusion.**

But here's the problem—**when you build an identity based on ego, you have to constantly maintain it.**

The Pressure of a Performative Life

You start posting for validation instead of sharing for yourself.

- It's no longer about what *you* enjoy—it's about what gets **likes, shares, and attention.**
- Every post becomes a **performance**, not an authentic expression.

You feel pressure to keep up the image even when you're struggling.

- You could be going through **real-life problems**, but ego tells you, *"Don't let them see you weak."*
- Instead of asking for support, you post something that makes it seem like you're **thriving.**

You start comparing yourself to others' online highlights, forgetting that it's **not real.**

- Social media **isn't reality.** It's a **filtered, edited, and curated** version of life.
- But ego convinces you that **everyone else has it figured out—except you.**

And the **worst part?**

The more you chase an **online version of yourself**, the more **disconnected** you become from your **real self.**

Because ego doesn't want authenticity—it wants **admiration.**

But real confidence doesn't come from **creating a persona.** It comes from **knowing who you actually are—without the need for external validation.**

How to Use Social Media in a Way That Benefits Your Mind and Soul

The answer isn't to **quit social media**—it's to **use it differently.**

Instead of letting it **control your ego**, you can shift how you interact with it:

1. Stop Chasing Validation—Post Without Attachment

The moment you post **without caring how it performs**, you **take back your power.**

Before posting, ask yourself:

- *Am I sharing this because I enjoy it, or because I want approval?*

- *Would I still post this if no one saw it?*

If the answer is **no**, your ego is running the show.
Try this instead:
- Post things because they **genuinely make you happy.**
- Share content **for self-expression**, not for validation.
- Detach your **worth** from likes, shares, or comments.

When you stop posting for **external approval**, you start using social media for **yourself—not for your ego.**

2. Remember That Social Media Isn't Real Life
People **curate** their lives online.
You're only seeing what they **want you to see.**
- No one is as **perfect, successful, or put-together** as they seem.
- Every highlight reel **hides struggles you don't see.**
- Comparison is **an illusion**—because you're comparing your *full* reality to someone else's *filtered* version.

When you remind yourself of this, comparison loses its power.
Practical ways to shift your mindset:
Scroll **consciously**, not mindlessly.

If a post **triggers** insecurity, remind yourself: *"This is just a moment, not their full reality."*

Spend **more time living** than consuming content about how others live.

3. Unfollow Accounts That Trigger Ego-Driven Thinking

If someone's content makes you feel:

Insecure about yourself

Inadequate in your achievements

Behind in life compared to others

Unfollow them. Period.

You control what you **consume.** Your feed should:

- Inspire you
- Motivate you
- Add value to your mindset and well-being

If it **feeds comparison, self-doubt, or negativity**, it's not worth your energy.

4. Focus on Real-Life Connections Over Digital Ones

No amount of **likes, followers, or online praise** can replace **genuine human connection.**

- **Call** a friend instead of texting.
- **Spend time** with people *without* posting about it.
- **Build memories** that don't need validation from the internet.

Ask yourself:

- *Am I prioritizing my real relationships, or just my digital ones?*
- *Would my life still feel fulfilling if I deleted social media tomorrow?*

If the answer is **no**, it's time to shift your focus.

Because at the end of the day?

Your real life is more important than your digital presence.

When Social Media Becomes an Identity Trap

The deeper danger of social media isn't just in comparison or validation—it's in **identity distortion**.

Ego uses social media as a mirror, but it's a **funhouse mirror**—one that shows a warped version of who you think you are and who you think you're supposed to be.

Over time, you stop being guided by your intuition, values, and real-life growth—and start letting **engagement metrics define your identity**:

- If people like your success story, you become the "success person."
- If people laugh at your jokes, you start performing instead of connecting.
- If people validate your pain, you might unintentionally stay in it—because being "relatable" gets more approval than healing ever will.

And that's the trap:

You become addicted to playing a role.

You become a character on your own feed.

You forget who you were before the camera turned on.

So ask yourself:

Are you still *being* who you are, or just playing the version of you that people liked most?

Because if social media turns you into a performance, your **real self starts fading in the background**—until you barely recognize them anymore.

Rebuilding Your Inner Compass

Social media keeps your eyes outward.

But growth requires looking inward.

That's why it's so important to **rebuild your inner compass**— so your self-worth isn't based on:

- Who's watching
- Who's clapping
- Or who's following

Start asking yourself:

- **What do I value when no one is watching?**
- **What would I still do, even if no one ever saw it?**
- **What makes me proud that has nothing to do with how it looks online?**

These are the questions that bring you back to *you*.

Reflective Exercise: Reclaim Your Real Self

Grab your journal and complete this 2-part reflection to check in with your relationship to social media and ego.

Part 1: Detox Your Ego

1. What's something I posted recently that felt more like performance than authenticity?

2. What was I hoping to get from it—validation, approval, attention, connection?

3. How did I feel when it didn't perform how I wanted (or when it did)?

4. What does that reaction tell me about where I've been outsourcing my self-worth?

Part 2: Reconnect With Your Truth

5. What kind of content would I share if I didn't care how it performed?

6. What would I *still* do, say, or create—even if no one ever liked it or saw it?

7. What are 3 things that make me proud of myself in real life, not online?

8. How can I remind myself daily that my real life matters more than my digital image?

Reminder:

You don't need to be seen to be valuable.

You don't need to go viral to be worthy.

And you don't need approval to live a life you're proud of.

Final Thoughts: Taking Back Control from Social Media

Social media **isn't evil**—but it becomes dangerous when it **feeds your ego instead of your soul.**

It was created to **connect people**, but too often, it disconnects you **from yourself.** It turns into a game of comparison, validation, and performance—one that never really ends.

So ask yourself: **Are you using social media, or is it using you? If you feel addicted to validation,** take a step back.

- Remind yourself that **your worth isn't tied to likes, comments, or shares.**
- Focus on posting for **expression, not approval.**
- Take breaks when needed—**you don't owe anyone constant access to you.**

If you feel pressured to prove yourself, remember that **real life matters more.**

- You don't have to capture every moment—some things are **meant to be lived, not posted.**
- You don't have to keep up with **what looks successful** online—focus on **what feels fulfilling in reality.**
- Your happiness **isn't measured** by an algorithm.

If you feel disconnected from who you really are, start focusing on what **fulfills you offline.**

- Spend time in places where social media **doesn't dictate your experience.**
- Invest in **real conversations, real moments, and real growth.**
- Make sure the life you're living **without the camera on** is one that truly makes you happy.

Because the moment you **stop needing social media** to feel valuable, **you become untouchable.**

You reclaim your confidence.

You reclaim your peace.

You reclaim your **power.**

Chapter 7: Blaming Others Instead of Looking Inward

Ego **loves** pointing fingers.

It makes you believe your problems are caused by **other people, external factors, or the world itself.**

- *"All men/women are the problem."*
- *"It's because of their zodiac sign."*
- *"It's a race/nationality thing."*
- *"People just don't understand me."*

Sound familiar? That's **ego talking.**

Ego convinces you that **you're never the issue.**

That it's always **them.**

That life would be easier if **people, circumstances, or society** just got their act together.

The Hard Truth?

The real issue **isn't** external—it's **ego twisting your perception.**

When ego controls your mindset, you start seeing **patterns that may not even exist.**

You start **blaming instead of reflecting.**

You start feeling **like a victim** instead of recognizing your own **power to change.**

And until you **recognize that**, you'll stay stuck in a **cycle of frustration, resentment, and missed growth.**

How Ego Creates Problems That Don't Exist

Ego thrives on **victim mentality.** It convinces you that you're **always the one being wronged** and that your struggles are the fault of other people, society, or some larger force beyond your control.

Instead of encouraging self-reflection, **ego distorts reality** to protect itself. It makes you see **patterns where there are none,** turning isolated experiences into *proof* of a bigger, external issue.

This mindset feels comforting because it removes the need for **self-accountability.** But in reality, it keeps you **stuck**—repeating the same cycles while blaming everything and everyone except yourself.

Here's how ego tricks you into creating problems that don't actually exist:

The "All Men/Women Are the Problem" Mindset

This is one of ego's favorite traps. When you get hurt in relationships, **ego doesn't want you to reflect**—it wants you to find an external reason to explain your pain.

How the Pattern Forms:

1. You experience **heartbreak or betrayal** in a relationship. Instead of processing what happened, ego convinces you:

- *"It's not me—it's them."*
- *"All men/women are the same."*

2. Your friend has a **bad dating experience** → Ego uses this as *confirmation* of your belief:

- *"See? It's a pattern."*

3. You start **viewing every interaction through this lens.** Even neutral or positive experiences get filtered through your past pain.

How This Keeps You Stuck:

You avoid **self-reflection** on why you keep choosing similar partners.

You ignore **your own red flags** in dating situations.

You push away **potentially great people** because they remind you of past experiences.

Reality Check:

Maybe it wasn't "all men/women." Maybe you **ignored red flags.**

Maybe you keep **attracting the same type** because you haven't healed your **own patterns.**

Maybe your **approach to relationships** needs to evolve.

But ego doesn't want to admit that—because that would mean taking **responsibility.**

Blaming Zodiac Signs Instead of Looking at Behavior

Astrology can be **fun** and insightful, but when ego gets involved, it becomes another **excuse to avoid personal accountability.**

How the Pattern Forms:

1. You meet someone who **acts shady** → Ego immediately blames their zodiac sign.

- *"Of course they ghosted me—they're a Gemini."*

2. You see a **viral post** about how [insert sign] is *"the worst"* →
Ego latches onto it as proof.

3. You start **writing people off** based on their sign instead of
actually observing their behavior.

How This Keeps You Stuck:

You assume **someone's actions** are because of their sign, instead
of their personal choices.

You ignore **red flags** if they don't match your pre-existing
beliefs.

You **miss out** on great connections because of *assumptions,* not
reality.

Reality Check:

Not everyone under the same sign acts the same way.
You're using astrology as a **shortcut to judgment** instead of actually
learning about people.

The **real issue isn't their sign**—it's how you're interpreting and
reacting to situations.

Ego wants **quick, easy answers.** It doesn't want to do the **deep
work of understanding** people on an individual level. But growth
requires **nuance, not labels.**

Turning Everything Into a Race/Nationality Issue

Another way ego **creates false patterns** is by filtering negative
experiences through **race, nationality, or culture.** Instead of
recognizing that **individuals are different,** ego convinces you that
one bad experience is part of a larger trend.

How the Pattern Forms:

1. You have a **negative experience** with someone → Ego tells you:

- *"It's because of where they're from.*

2. You hear a **stereotype** about that group → Ego **clings to it as truth.**

3. Now, you **view every interaction through bias**, assuming all people from that background behave the same way.

How This Keeps You Stuck:

You form **biased opinions** based on limited experiences.

You create **division** instead of understanding.

You make **decisions based on assumptions** rather than reality.

Reality Check:

Was it actually their **race/nationality**, or were they just a **bad person?**

Have you interacted with **enough people** to make a fair judgment?

Is this belief **helping you grow**, or keeping you **stuck in resentment?**

Ego **loves black-and-white thinking.** It doesn't like **nuance**— because nuance requires **effort and self-awareness.**

But when you **let go of ego-based biases**, you start seeing people for **who they truly are**—not what your ego assumes they are.

The Bottom Line? Ego Creates Illusions.

Ego is **always looking for a way to avoid self-reflection.**

Instead of asking:

- *"What can I learn from this?"*
- *"How can I grow from this?"*

Ego asks:

- *"Who can I blame for this?"*

It convinces you that **your problems are external,** when in reality, the biggest obstacle might be **your own mindset.**

The moment you **stop searching for patterns that don't exist** and start **taking accountability**, you break free from ego's illusions—and start seeing the world *clearly* for the first time.

Assuming Everyone Thinks Like You

Ego limits your perspective by trapping you in your own bubble. It convinces you that your way of thinking is the *default*—that anyone who doesn't think, speak, or act like you must be wrong, weird, or less evolved.

How the Pattern Forms:

1. You grow up in a certain environment—maybe a specific culture, religion, community, or even a certain socioeconomic background. Ego internalizes this environment as "normal."

- "This is just how people are."
- "Everyone knows this."

2. You meet someone who behaves differently—whether in conversation, values, or even body language. Ego feels *threatened* by the unfamiliar and judges it.

- "That's rude."

102

- "Why would anyone do that?"
- "They're not making sense."

3. Instead of being curious or open, ego shuts down the moment something challenges its version of reality.

How This Keeps You Stuck:

You misinterpret others' actions and intentions because you filter them through your own lens.

You dismiss valuable ideas, wisdom, or perspectives just because they don't match yours.

You lose opportunities to grow, connect, or expand because ego would rather feel "right" than evolve.

Reality Check:

Not everyone grew up where you did.

Not everyone had your parents, your education, your culture, or your access.

People speak, move, and process differently—not because they're wrong, but because they were shaped by different experiences.

Your way is *a* way—not *the* way. The moment you accept that, the world opens up. You become more observant, more compassionate, and more connected.

Ego says: "Everyone should think like me."

Growth says: "Let me understand why they think differently."

Letting go of the ego's belief that your view is the only valid one is how real perspective begins. It's not just about being open-minded—it's about being *self-aware* enough to realize that your mind is only one of billions.

Using Environment as an Excuse Not to Try

Ego doesn't just limit your perspective—it also gives you permission to stop trying. When your worldview is small, ego tells you that success, knowledge, or growth is something *other people* have access to, but not you.

How the Pattern Forms:

1. You grow up in a disadvantaged area, surrounded by struggle or limited resources. Ego internalizes this environment as a *barrier*, not a starting point.

- "I'm from here, so people like me don't make it."
- "No one helps us."
- "We don't have the same opportunities."

2. You look around and see people who are also stuck—and ego uses this as proof.

- "See? Everyone around me is struggling, too. That's just how it is."
- "If they're not trying, why should I?"

3. You stop looking *for* solutions and start looking *at* problems.

Instead of asking, "How can I use what I have?"
You ask, "Why don't I have what they have?"

How This Keeps You Stuck:

You start to believe that effort doesn't matter.

You convince yourself that success is reserved for people in better environments.

You overlook the tools you already have because they don't look like the tools you expected.

Reality Check:

That kid may be from a poor neighborhood—but he's walking around with a smartphone.

A device that holds more knowledge than most libraries in human history.

He has access to *information, education, how-tos, tutorials, free courses, job listings,* and *connection to people* across the globe.

But ego convinces him he's powerless—because it doesn't want to admit that what's missing isn't resources...it's perspective.

He doesn't need someone to come save him.

He needs to *see* himself as someone who's already equipped to take the first step.

Ego says: "I don't have what I need."

Truth says: "You do. You just haven't realized it yet."

When ego is in control, it turns your story into a cage. When *you* take control, that same story becomes the reason you rise.

How to Break Free from Ego-Based Blame and See Things Clearly

The key to breaking free? **Radical self-awareness.**

Ego **protects itself** by convincing you that your struggles are **caused by other people, external circumstances, or**

uncontrollable forces. It filters reality so that you only see **what confirms your beliefs,** making it easy to justify blame and avoid self-reflection.

But **here's the truth:** The patterns you experience **won't change until you do.**

Instead of blaming external factors, start **challenging your own perspective:**

- *"Am I looking at the full picture, or just the parts that support my belief?"*
- *"What role did I play in this situation?"*
- *"Am I projecting my personal experience onto an entire group of people?"*

The moment you start **asking different questions,** you start getting **different answers.**

1. Recognize the Pattern

The first step to breaking ego-based blame is **becoming aware of when it's happening.**

Ego loves to create **false patterns** to explain why things happen, even when those patterns don't actually exist.

Ask yourself:

- Do I often **generalize people** based on a few bad experiences?
- Do I **reject personal accountability** and always blame outside factors?
- Do I **cling to stereotypes** or external reasons for why things happen?

- Do I **focus on what others did to me** instead of how I contributed to the situation?

Example:

"Every time I try to open up, people hurt me." → *Blame-based thinking*

"Am I choosing emotionally unavailable people? Am I ignoring red flags?" → *Growth-based thinking*

"I never get good opportunities because the system is rigged." → *Blame-based thinking*

"Am I actively positioning myself for better opportunities? What can I do differently?" → *Growth-based thinking*

The **more you recognize these patterns**, the easier it becomes to **interrupt them before they control you.**

2. Shift from Blame to Reflection

Blame **feels good in the moment** because it takes the weight off of you. But if you want to actually **grow**, you have to shift from **blame to reflection.**

Every time you catch yourself **blaming someone or something**, flip the script:

Instead of "People always do this to me," try:

"Why do I keep ending up in these situations?"

"What can I change about my approach?"

"How can I stop repeating this cycle?"

Instead of "It's because of their sign/gender/background," try:

"Was this actually about that, or was it just about them as a person?"

"Am I using labels as an excuse to avoid personal growth?"

"What happens if I let go of these assumptions?"

Instead of "Nobody supports me," try:

"Am I surrounding myself with the right people?"

"Do I clearly communicate my needs?"

"Am I waiting for external validation instead of validating myself?"

Ego wants you to **stay in victim mode**. Reflection forces you to **step into your power.**

When you shift from **"They did this to me"** to **"How can I grow from this?"**, you start making real changes in your life.

3. Accept That Growth Requires Self-Accountability

This is the hardest step—because it means acknowledging that **some of your struggles come from your own decisions, patterns, and perceptions.**

And that's uncomfortable.

But discomfort = **growth.**

Ask yourself:

- If I **keep having the same negative experiences**, what can I change about my approach?

- If I **keep attracting the same kind of people**, what does that say about my boundaries, self-worth, and energy?
- If I **keep feeling stuck**, am I actually putting in the effort to change, or just complaining about my circumstances?

When you **take ownership** of your patterns, you stop **waiting for the world to change** and start **changing yourself.**

But here's the powerful part:

When you shift **your mindset**, your experiences change. When you stop **blaming others**, you start growing in ways you never thought possible.

When you take **accountability**, you gain control over your own future.

Ego wants you **stuck.** Awareness **sets you free.**

And the moment you stop looking **outward** for the problem and start looking **inward** for the solution, you take back your **power to create the life you want.**

The Illusion of Blame Feels Safer Than the Truth

Here's the real reason ego loves blame so much:

Blame is easier than responsibility.

- It's easier to say "they were toxic" than to admit you ignored red flags.
- It's easier to say "they always let me down" than to admit you overextend and expect people to save you.
- It's easier to say "they judged me" than to admit you're still healing from your own insecurities.

Blame protects your pride. Responsibility exposes your patterns. But growth?

Growth only happens when you're willing to **stop protecting your ego and start protecting your evolution.**

Because here's the truth: **You can't change what you refuse to own.**

And when you *don't* own your part in a pattern, it repeats. New people, same energy. New job, same problems. New city, same emptiness.

But when you take radical accountability? You rewrite the story—on your terms.

Reflective Exercise: From Blame to Breakthrough

Use this journal prompt to uncover where ego may be keeping you stuck in blame—and how to shift into real power.

Step 1: Identify the Situation

Think of something you've been blaming others for. It could be recent or something you've carried for a long time.

Write it down:

"I've been blaming _____ for _____."

Step 2: Unpack the Blame

Now ask yourself:

- What exactly did I believe they did wrong?
- How have I repeated this story to myself or others?

- How does holding onto this blame make me feel powerful, safe, or "right"?

Step 3: Take Honest Inventory

Now get honest. Ask yourself:

- Did I ignore red flags?
- Did I communicate my needs clearly?
- Did I react emotionally instead of reflecting first?
- Did I have unrealistic expectations of this person/situation?

Step 4: Choose the Shift

Now shift the narrative:

- "Even though that hurt me, I choose to look at how I showed up, too."
- "I can learn from this instead of just resenting it."
- "My growth is more important than being right."

Step 5: Write a New Story

Complete this sentence:

"From this experience, I now choose to _____."

Examples:

- Set better boundaries.
- Listen to my intuition earlier.
- Speak up instead of staying silent.
- Stop giving chances to people who show me they don't deserve them.

The Cost of Staying in Blame

If blame is your comfort zone, reflection is your breakthrough.
But here's the cost of staying in blame:

- You stay powerless.
- You stay bitter.
- You stay stuck in situations that keep repeating.

The question isn't: *"Whose fault is it?"*
The real question is:

"Am I more committed to being right or being free?"

Because blame might give you the last word,
—but accountability gives you your life back.

Final Thoughts: Reclaiming Your Power from Ego-Based Blame

Ego wants you to believe the problem is **always outside of you.**
Because as long as you believe that, you'll:

- **Never change**
- **Never grow**
- **Never take control**

But the moment you turn the focus **inward?**

- You stop seeing yourself as a **victim.**
- You stop wasting energy on **things you can't control.**
- You start making **real, conscious changes** that improve your life.

True power doesn't come from **blaming, complaining, or pointing fingers.**

It comes from **owning your mindset, your choices, and your actions.**

And once you do that? **You free yourself.**

Chapter 8: Breaking Free from Ego-Driven Comparison

Comparison is one of **ego's favorite weapons.** It tricks you into believing that your **worth is measured by how you stack up against others.**

It makes you feel like you're constantly in a **competition**—whether you signed up for one or not.

- **Someone else is doing better than you?** → Ego whispers, *"You're falling behind."*

- **Someone else gets praised?** → Ego says, *"Why them and not you?"*

- **Someone disagrees with you?** → Ego screams, *"Prove them wrong!"*

Ego thrives on **comparison** because comparison keeps you **distracted from your own path.**

How Ego Uses Comparison to Keep You Stuck
1. Ego Makes You Feel Like You're Always Behind

Ego convinces you that success is a **race**—one where you're **never moving fast enough.**

- You see someone else get promoted, and instead of feeling happy for them, ego whispers: *"Why aren't you at that level yet?"*

- You scroll through social media and see someone traveling, buying a house, or hitting a big milestone, and ego says: *"You should be doing that too."*

Reality check:
You are not on the same timeline as anyone else.
Growth is **not linear**—your journey is your own.
What's meant for you **will not miss you**—but it won't look like someone else's success.
The moment you stop **measuring your progress by someone else's timeline**, you start living on **your own terms**.

2. Ego Makes Other People's Success Feel Like Your Failure

Ego **doesn't like sharing the spotlight.** When someone else wins, ego wants to know: *"What about me?"*

- A friend gets engaged? Ego says, *"Why haven't you found someone yet?"*
- Someone gets recognition at work? Ego says, *"They don't deserve that more than me."*
- A business owner you know is thriving? Ego says, *"They got lucky."*

Comparison makes you see **someone else's moment as a reflection of your own worth.** But their success has **nothing to do with you.**

Reality check:

Someone else winning does not mean you're losing. The only thing another person's success should do is **inspire you— not threaten you.**

You don't need to **dim their light** to make yours shine.

When you celebrate other people's success **without resentment,** you create space for your **own abundance.**

3. Ego Makes You Chase Approval Instead of Purpose

Ego **wants validation** more than it wants meaning. That's why it pushes you to **prove yourself** rather than **be yourself.**

- You start **setting goals** based on what looks impressive instead of what actually makes you happy.
- You feel the need to **outshine** others instead of focusing on your own progress.
- You make decisions based on **how they'll be perceived** instead of what's actually right for you.

Example:

You feel pressure to buy expensive things—not because you want them, but because you think they'll make you *look* successful.

You take a job you don't like—not because it aligns with your passion, but because it sounds *impressive.*

You post something on social media—not because it's meaningful, but because you *need engagement.*

Reality check:

The moment you stop **seeking validation**, you start finding fulfillment.

Real confidence isn't about **looking successful**—it's about being **at peace with yourself.**

You don't need **to prove anything** to anyone.

When you stop **letting comparison dictate your choices,** you gain the **freedom to actually live.**

How Ego Makes You Obsessed with Proving Your Worth Instead of Living Your Truth

Ego **doesn't care about happiness**—it cares about **winning.**

That's why it constantly pushes you to:

Compete with people who aren't even in your lane.

Why are you comparing yourself to someone with a completely different life path?

Why are you measuring your success against someone whose goals, resources, or experiences are nothing like yours?

Chase success that doesn't even fulfill you.

Are you building the life you actually want, or just the one that looks impressive to others?

Are you pursuing your dreams, or just the ones that society says are "worthy" of respect?

Feel insecure about things that don't actually matter.

Is this your insecurity, or is it something society told you to care about?

Would this even bother you if there was no one around to judge you for it?

Ego doesn't want you to **be at peace**—it wants you to **fight to be seen as valuable.**

It tricks you into believing that your **self-worth is something you have to prove**, rather than something you already have.

The result?

- You chase **titles, status, and external validation** instead of fulfillment.
- You constantly feel like you're in **competition with everyone around you.**
- You measure your life based on **what it looks like to others** instead of how it actually *feels* to you.

But the moment you **stop trying to prove yourself?**
You start **actually living.**

You stop **seeking approval** and start **seeking joy.** You define **success on your own terms.**

Signs Ego Is Keeping You Stuck in Comparison Mode

If you're caught in **ego-driven comparison**, you might recognize these signs:

You feel like other people's success means you're behind.

- Instead of seeing success as **abundant and limitless**, you treat it like a **competition.**

118

- You believe that if someone else wins, it means there's **less for you.**

You struggle to celebrate others without feeling inadequate.
- When someone else is thriving, you feel like **you're failing.**
- Instead of seeing inspiration, you feel **threatened.**

You base your self-worth on external validation (likes, attention, recognition).
- You feel **amazing** when you're getting praise—but empty when no one's watching.
- You crave **acknowledgment** because without it, you feel like you're *not enough.*

You feel pressure to "prove" you're successful, smart, or attractive instead of just being yourself.
- You're more focused on **how things appear** than how they *actually feel.*
- You're exhausted from trying to **keep up an image** rather than just **existing in your truth.**

If any of this sounds familiar, it's time to **detach from ego's grip on comparison.**

Because your worth **isn't something you need to prove.**

It's something you already **own.**

The Freedom of Not Taking Everything Personally

The biggest reason people get stuck in **ego-driven comparison?**
They take **everything** personally.

- **Someone else is doing well?** → Ego sees it as a **threat.**
- **Someone doesn't praise you?** → Ego whispers, *"You must not be enough."*
- **Someone disagrees with you?** → Ego makes you feel **attacked, unheard, or invalidated.**

But here's the truth:

Other people's **success** has nothing to do with your path.

Other people's **opinions** are reflections of their own experiences, not your worth.

Other people's **actions** are shaped by their own reality, not yours.

How Taking Things Personally Keeps You Stuck

Ego tricks you into believing that **everything happening around you is somehow about you.**

- Someone is short with you? Ego says, *"They must not respect me."*
- A friend doesn't respond to your text? Ego says, *"They're ignoring me on purpose."*
- Someone chooses a different path than you? Ego says, *"They think they're better than me."*

But most of the time?

People are caught up in their **own lives, thoughts, and struggles.**

Their actions are based on **their personal circumstances—not a direct reflection of you.**

The way people behave often has **nothing to do with you at all.**

Yet when ego takes over, you waste time **overanalyzing and reacting** to things that were never about you in the first place.

What Happens When You Stop Taking Things Personally?

You stop feeling threatened by other people's success.

You shift from *comparison* to *inspiration.*

Instead of seeing someone's win as proof that you're losing, you realize:

"If they can do it, so can I."

You stop feeling the need to prove yourself to anyone.
You no longer make decisions out of fear of judgment.
You trust yourself, your path, and your timing—without needing validation.

You stop reacting emotionally to things that don't actually matter.
You learn to *pause* instead of reacting impulsively.
You let go of unnecessary drama because you realize **not everything deserves your energy.**

The truth is, **there is no competition.**

121

Other people aren't *against* you—they're just *for* themselves.

The only person you need to **impress, prove yourself to, and compete with?**

You.

And the moment you stop taking things personally, you gain **the ultimate freedom**—the ability to **live for yourself, not for comparison, approval, or ego.**

How to Step Away from External Validation and Embrace Real Self-Worth

True **self-worth** comes from inside—but **ego wants you to chase it outside.**

Ego convinces you that your value is something you must **earn through approval, praise, and recognition.** It keeps you **hooked on external validation,** making you feel like you're only as worthy as the last compliment, like, or achievement.

But the truth?

You don't need validation from anyone else to be valuable.

You don't need to "keep up" to be worthy.

You don't need to prove anything to anyone.

So how do you break the cycle and **embrace real self-worth?**

1. Shift Your Mindset from Competition to Creation

Ego makes you **compete.** It tells you that your value is determined by how you compare to others. But real fulfillment comes from **creating the life you actually want,** not chasing someone else's version of success.

Instead of thinking:

"I need to prove I'm better." → **Think:** *"I need to create a life that feels good to me."*

"I need to keep up with them." → **Think:** *"I need to focus on my own path."*

Reality check:

Your journey is not meant to look like anyone else's.

The moment you focus on **your own growth**, comparison loses its grip on you.

The more you **create what aligns with your soul**, the less you care about proving yourself to anyone else.

When you focus on **creating the life you want**, you stop worrying about **what everyone else is doing.**

2. Validate Yourself First

One of the biggest reasons people get **trapped in external validation?** They never learned how to **validate themselves first.**

Instead of waiting for:

Social media likes → **Ask yourself:** *Do I like what I'm doing?*

Praise from others → **Ask yourself:** *Am I proud of myself?*

Approval from society → **Ask yourself:** *Does this actually make me happy?*

The more you validate **yourself internally**, the less you rely on **external validation.**

Practical ways to start validating yourself:

- **Practice self-acknowledgment.** Instead of waiting for someone else to recognize your efforts, take a moment to acknowledge your own growth.
- **Celebrate small wins.** You don't need a huge accomplishment to feel proud of yourself. Every step forward matters.
- **Make choices based on what feels right to you.** If you're making a decision **just to impress someone else**, pause and ask: *"Would I still do this if no one was watching?"*

True self-worth comes from within. **No amount of likes, applause, or approval can replace the confidence that comes from trusting yourself.**

3. Let Go of the Need to "Win"

Ego tells you life is a **race**. That you need to:
- **"Win" success** to feel valuable.
- **"Win" relationships** to feel worthy.
- **"Win" respect** to feel important.

But what if you stopped trying to **win against others** and just **focused on living well?**

What if you pursued success because you enjoyed the journey, not just to impress others?

What if you worked on yourself because it felt good, not because you wanted to be better than someone else?

What if you let go of competition mode and focused on alignment mode?

Competition mode: Chasing validation, proving yourself, constantly comparing.

Alignment mode: Choosing what feels right, trusting yourself, growing at your own pace.

Reality check:

You don't need to "win" anything to be worthy.

The real measure of success isn't how you compare—it's how aligned you are with **your own values, goals, and happiness.**

The only person you ever needed to impress was **yourself.**

And once you detach from the need to **win against others**, you finally become **free to live for yourself.**

The Trap of Competing With a Story You Don't Know

Social media, gossip, and surface-level success make it easy to compare. But here's what ego doesn't tell you:

You're competing with *a curated version* of someone's life.

That person you're comparing yourself to?

- You don't know what they gave up to get there.
- You don't know what they're dealing with behind the scenes.
- You don't know what they *feel* when the lights go off.

Ego zooms in on the one shiny part and says, "Why not you?" But it never considers whether you'd want the full picture.

Reality check:

You might not want their whole life—you just want their *highlight reel.*

When you realize that, the urge to compete starts to fade. Because you understand you're comparing your *behind-the-scenes* to their *best-of.*

How Comparison Silences Your Inner Child

Your inner child isn't interested in comparison—it's interested in joy.

But the more ego takes over, the quieter that voice becomes.

- As a kid, you didn't care who was "winning." You just wanted to *play, explore, and express.*
- But now? You post and wait for approval. You chase status. You second-guess your joy because it doesn't look "successful."

That's the cost of comparison—it disconnects you from your natural self.

Your inner child doesn't want to be impressive. It wants to be *alive.*

The more you measure yourself by others, the more you abandon the part of you that never needed to prove anything at all.

Bring that version of you back.

The one who created just to create.

The one who laughed without worrying if it was "cool."

The one who felt free.

That's who you're returning to when you let go of comparison.

The Trap of Competing With a Story You Don't Know

Social media, gossip, and surface-level success make it easy to compare. But here's what ego doesn't tell you:

You're competing with *a curated version* of someone's life.

That person you're comparing yourself to?

- You don't know what they gave up to get there.
- You don't know what they're dealing with behind the scenes.
- You don't know what they *feel* when the lights go off.

Ego zooms in on the one shiny part and says, "Why not you?" But it never considers whether you'd want the full picture.

Reality check:

You might not want their whole life—you just want their *highlight reel.*

When you realize that, the urge to compete starts to fade. Because you understand you're comparing your *behind-the-scenes* to their *best-of.*

How Comparison Silences Your Inner Child

Your inner child isn't interested in comparison—it's interested in joy.

But the more ego takes over, the quieter that voice becomes.

- As a kid, you didn't care who was "winning." You just wanted to *play, explore, and express.*
- But now? You post and wait for approval. You chase status. You second-guess your joy because it doesn't look "successful."

That's the cost of comparison—it disconnects you from your natural self.

Your inner child doesn't want to be impressive. It wants to be *alive*.

The more you measure yourself by others, the more you abandon the part of you that never needed to prove anything at all.

Bring that version of you back.

The one who created just to create.

The one who laughed without worrying if it was "cool."

The one who felt free.

That's who you're returning to when you let go of comparison.

Reflective Exercise: Shifting Out of Comparison Mode

This 5-step journaling prompt is designed to help you break free from ego-driven comparison and realign with your own truth.

Step 1: Name the Comparison Trigger What specific moment or person triggered your comparison?

- Who or what are you comparing yourself to?
- What did they have, do, or achieve that made you feel "less than"?

Step 2: Identify the Emotion Underneath What did that comparison actually make you feel?

(Examples: jealousy, shame, frustration, insecurity, pressure)

Be honest. No judgment—just awareness.

Step 3: Ask the Real Questions Now dig deeper:

- Do I actually want what they have, or do I just think I *should* want it?
- Is this aligned with my values—or just something I feel pressured to chase?
- Would I even want their lifestyle if I had to live all parts of it?

Step 4: Reconnect With Your Path What makes *your* journey uniquely yours?

- What are you proud of that has nothing to do with anyone else?
- What would success look and feel like for *you*, if no one else was watching?

Step 5: Reframe the Trigger Into Truth Turn the trigger into a grounded affirmation:

Instead of: "They're ahead of me."

Try: "I'm exactly where I need to be."

Instead of: "I should be further."

Try: "I trust my timing and my path."

Instead of: "I'm falling behind."

Try: "There is no race. I'm building a life that's mine."

129

Final Thoughts: True Confidence Comes from Letting Go

Ego tells you that confidence comes from **being better than others.**

That you need to **outshine, outperform, and outdo** to be valuable.

But **real confidence?**

It comes from **not caring how you measure up to anyone at all.**

True confidence is:

Knowing your worth without needing validation.

Trusting your path without comparing it to others.

Feeling secure in yourself, even when no one is watching.

When you stop **comparing, proving, and competing**, you gain something even better: **peace.**

Because when you're **truly secure in yourself?**

You stop seeking validation. → You don't need others to **confirm your worth.**

You stop feeling threatened by others. → You celebrate people's success **without feeling behind.**

You stop living for external approval. → You start **living for you.**

And that's real freedom.

Chapter 9: Ego in Friendships – The Unspoken Battle

Friendship is supposed to be your soft place to land.
Your peace. Your people. Your chosen family.
But sometimes... the bond gets weird. The vibe shifts.
Suddenly, things feel off and no one knows why — or no one wants to say it.

And more often than not? That tension isn't just about them. It's ego. Yours or theirs — or both.

We don't talk enough about ego in friendships. We expect the drama in romance, the politics at work, the tension in family. But in close friendships?

Ego plays chess silently.

You start to feel competitive.

You start downplaying your wins or secretly hoping theirs don't outshine yours.

You question your worth when they're thriving. You feel left out, replaced, or like you're not "needed" anymore — and instead of addressing it, you detach and act like you're "just busy."

But here's the truth: **jealousy, validation-seeking, and constant comparison don't come from friendship — they come from ego.**

The Jealousy No One Admits

It's hard to admit when we feel jealous of someone we love. It makes us feel small, petty, or fake.

But jealousy is human — it's what we do with it that matters. When your friend is glowing up, the ego whispers:

- "Why not me?"
- "They're forgetting about you."
- "You'll never catch up."
- "You're falling behind."

Suddenly, it's not *their* win — it's your *loss*. That's ego twisting the moment into a threat. But your friend's success doesn't take anything from you. It doesn't change your worth. It doesn't put you behind.

You can celebrate others without shrinking yourself. You can feel your feelings and still show up with love.

If you let ego speak, you'll pull away, act weird, or try to "one-up" them instead of supporting them. If you let love speak, you'll be proud, inspired, and excited — because *your circle's wins are your wins too*.

The Validation Trap

Sometimes ego doesn't want attention — it wants *proof* that you're important. It wants reassurance that you matter in their life. That you're still needed. That you're still the favorite.

You start keeping score:

- Who texts first.
- Who shows up more.
- Who gets praised in the group chat.

And if you don't feel seen, ego screams: "They don't value you! Pull back. Make them chase you. They'll realize what they lost."

But here's the truth: validation that has to be forced or tested is *never real connection.*

Real friendship isn't about being the center of attention — it's about being in a safe space where love isn't a competition.

How to Stop Comparing and Start Connecting Authentically

Want to protect your friendships from ego's silent sabotage? Here's how:

Shift from comparison to curiosity.

Instead of "Why are they winning and I'm not?" ask, "What can I learn from their path?" Your friends can *inspire* you without intimidating you.

Communicate instead of withdrawing.

If something's bothering you — say it. Not in a dramatic, accusatory way. In a "Hey, I've been feeling a little off lately, can we talk?" way. That's maturity. That's care.

Remind yourself: there's enough room for everyone to thrive.

Friendship is not a game of limited seats. Your light doesn't dim just because someone else is shining bright.

Celebrate without self-doubt.

If your friend wins, celebrate loudly. Don't overthink it. Don't make it about you. That energy will come back around when it's your turn.

Recognizing When Ego is the Real Problem

It's not always them. It's not always a "vibe." Sometimes *your* ego is the one pulling you back, making you feel unseen, unwanted, or triggered.

Ask yourself:

- Am I actually being excluded... or am I assuming the worst?
- Am I communicating... or expecting them to read my mind?
- Am I genuinely happy for them... or silently competing?
- Am I supporting them the way I want to be supported?

When you pause to reflect, ego gets quieter — and your ability to connect gets louder.

When Nothing's *Wrong*... But Something Feels Off

Not every friendship shift comes with betrayal, drama, or a falling out.

Sometimes... it's subtle.

You start texting less.

You second-guess what you say around them.

You downplay your wins so they don't feel some type of way — or so you don't get judged for "doing too much."

You replay small moments, wondering if they were shade or if you're just being sensitive.

And little by little, ego starts whispering in the background:

- "They don't really care about you."
- "Don't reach out — let them miss you."
- "Protect your energy. They're probably jealous."
- "You don't need them anyway."

But what if none of that is true?

What if you're not being excluded — you're just letting assumptions lead?

What if your silence is creating the exact disconnection you're afraid of?

What if this friendship is still real — but your ego's unspoken fears are warping how you experience it?

This is where the danger of unspoken ego really shows up: not in betrayal, but in miscommunication. In overthinking. In assumptions. In emotional armor you didn't even realize you were wearing.

That's why self-awareness is key.

Because sometimes it's not about "cutting people off."

Sometimes, it's about checking in with yourself — and cleaning the lens you're seeing them through.

When Ego Turns a Friend Into a Secret Rival

Not every friendship ends in a blow-up. Some slowly erode because one person is secretly competing while pretending to care.

You might not even notice it at first.

But over time, the signs start stacking up:

- They make passive-aggressive jokes that embarrass you when you're around others — especially in front of men.
- They "tease" you, but the humor always cuts a little too deep.
- They act cool and composed when you're emotional, just to make you look "immature" by comparison.
- They only lift you up when no one's watching — but when attention is on the both of you, they subtly push you down to shine.

It's not always blatant. That's what makes it confusing. They'll say *they're just joking,* or that *you're being sensitive.* But if it consistently makes you feel small, uncomfortable, or off... trust that.

That's ego — theirs, not yours.

Because when someone sees you as competition instead of community, the friendship was never real to begin with.

True friends don't need to one-up you. They don't need to play it cool while throwing you under the bus for male validation. They don't need to make you the punchline just to make themselves feel more secure.

Real friendship is love, not strategy.

If someone constantly needs to feel like "the mature one," "the desirable one," or "the more put-together one" — they're not trying to connect with you. They're trying to outrank you.

You're allowed to walk away from that dynamic with no explanation.

You're allowed to stop laughing off the comments that actually hurt.

You're allowed to stop playing nice with people who play dirty in subtle ways.

It's not a loss — it's clarity.

Friendship Ego Audit: Is It Them, Or Is It Ego?

This isn't about blaming anyone — it's about checking in with *yourself*. Because at the end of the day, how you *feel* in someone's presence matters more than what they *say*. Someone might not mean any harm... but that doesn't mean the connection is healthy for you right now.

Take a moment and ask yourself these questions with honesty and compassion:

1. Do I feel drained, anxious, or "less than" after spending time with this friend — even if they didn't say or do anything outright harmful?

2. Am I constantly comparing myself to them, or feeling like I need to prove something around them?

3. Do I feel like I can be my *full self* in this friendship — or am I performing, shrinking, or overexplaining?

4. Have I tried to communicate when something feels off, or have I been silently withdrawing and letting ego fill in the blanks?

5. Am I genuinely happy for their wins, or do I secretly feel bitter, insecure, or forgotten?

6. Do I trust them with my vulnerability — or do I keep it surface-level to protect myself?

7. Have they actually done anything that violated my boundaries — or am I triggered by my own inner wounds, past friendships, or unmet needs?

8. Do I feel seen, supported, and respected — or just tolerated and "kept around"?

Now ask yourself the most important question:

Regardless of their intent... does this friendship feel like alignment, or does it feel like emotional work I didn't sign up for?

You're allowed to outgrow connections.

You're allowed to keep people in your heart but not in your everyday life.

You're allowed to walk away from what drains you — even if there was no big betrayal.

Just make sure you're not confusing ego's fear of being left out with your soul's need for peace.

Affirmation Drop: Real Friendship Doesn't Feel Like Competition

Say these out loud, write them down, or repeat them to yourself when ego starts creeping in:

- I don't need to compete where I feel complete.
- My friends' success doesn't dim my own light.
- I celebrate others without questioning my own worth.

- I am safe to be vulnerable and honest in the right friendships.
- I don't chase validation — I choose connection.
- I can love people from a distance and still protect my peace.
- I release the need to be "needed" and embrace being respected.
- I honor the friendships that feel like home — and I lovingly let go of the ones that don't.

Your friendships deserve the version of you that's present, honest, and grounded — not the version that's silently competing, doubting, or keeping score.

And if someone's ego is the one blocking connection? You'll recognize it faster when yours isn't in the way.

Part 3: The Path to Inner Peace

Transcending the Ego

Now that you've seen how ego shows up and how the world keeps feeding it, it's time to take your power back.

This part is about remembering who you are *beneath* the ego—beneath the fear, the control, the overthinking, and the need to prove anything to anyone. It's about getting quiet enough to hear your inner voice again... the one that's been there the whole time, just waiting for you to listen.

Transcending the ego doesn't mean you never feel triggered again or that you become some perfectly enlightened being. It means you start choosing peace over pride. Stillness over chaos. Truth over illusion. Every time you choose presence over reaction, you break another ego pattern. And that's where freedom begins.

This is the chapter where you come home to yourself. No masks. No defense mechanisms. Just you—and a version of peace that no one can take away.

Chapter 10: The Power of Letting Go

Letting go is the **ultimate power move.**

Not because it makes you **weak.**

Not because it means **giving up.**

But because **holding on**—to ego-driven thoughts, emotions, and expectations—is what's actually keeping you **stuck.**

Ego wants control. It wants certainty. It wants things to go **exactly as it expects.** And when they don't? It resists. It holds on. It creates stress, overthinking, and frustration.

But when you **let go?**

You stop forcing things that aren't meant for you. You stop seeking validation from people who don't matter. You stop wasting energy on things you can't change.

Letting go is not weakness—it's power.

Why Letting Go of Ego is the Key to Emotional Freedom

Ego traps you in **mental and emotional weight** you don't need to carry.

It convinces you that **holding on** is a form of strength. But in reality, **letting go** is what sets you free.

Here's how ego keeps you trapped:

It holds onto grudges because it hates admitting it was wrong.

- Ego wants to be **right** at all costs—even at the expense of your peace.
- It convinces you that **forgiveness is weakness**, when in reality, it's **liberation.**

It clings to expectations because it fears uncertainty.

- Ego wants **control**—it wants everything to go exactly as planned.
- When things don't go as expected, it **creates frustration, anxiety, and disappointment.**

It obsesses over what people think because it seeks validation.

- Ego makes you **hyper-aware of others' opinions**—because it wants approval.
- It convinces you that your **worth depends on how you're perceived.**

But the moment you **let go?**

You free up mental space.

- You stop replaying old arguments, regrets, and what-ifs.
- Your mind becomes **lighter, clearer, and more present.**

You gain emotional peace.

- You stop taking things **personally** and reacting from ego.
- You experience **calm, acceptance, and emotional stability.**

You start living instead of overthinking.

- You stop trying to **control everything** and start enjoying what *is*.
- You trust life more, stress less, and **flow with what's meant for you.**

Letting Go Doesn't Mean You Stop Caring—It Means You Stop Clinging

It doesn't mean you stop having **goals, standards, or emotions.**

It doesn't mean you let people **walk all over you.**

It doesn't mean you don't **work toward what you want.**

It means you **detach from unhealthy attachments.**

It means you **release what no longer serves you.**

It means you **focus on what actually matters, instead of what ego fixates on.**

Letting go isn't **losing**—it's **winning back your freedom.**

How Ego Creates Stress, Overthinking, and Unhappiness

Ego **hates uncertainty.** It craves **control, certainty, and a perfect storyline** that makes you feel important, successful, and in charge.

But life **doesn't work that way.**

Ego's obsession with **controlling everything** only creates:

Unnecessary stress

Endless overthinking

Constant unhappiness

Here's how ego keeps you stuck:

Overanalyzing Every Situation

Ego makes you:

- Replay conversations in your head, trying to figure out *what they really meant.*

- Obsess over how people **see you** or what they **think about you.**
- Predict **worst-case scenarios** that haven't even happened.

Example:

"Did they ignore my message on purpose?"

"Why did they say it like that?"

"What if they don't like me anymore?"

Reality check:

Most people **aren't thinking about you as much as you think they are.**

Not everything needs to be analyzed. Some things are just what they are. **The more you overanalyze, the less you actually live.**

Holding Onto Past Mistakes

Ego **hates being wrong.** It doesn't want to accept that the **past is over.**

So it **clings to regret, shame, and guilt**—constantly reminding you of what you *"should have done differently."*

Example:

"I can't believe I said that."

"If I had done this differently, everything would be better now."

"I ruined my chances."

Reality check:

The past cannot be changed—but your mindset can. Holding onto regret doesn't **fix anything**, it just **weighs you down.**

The only way to **heal from the past is to learn from it and move forward.**

Worrying About the Future

Ego wants **certainty**—so it constantly tries to **predict and control** the future.

But instead of preparing you, it just creates **anxiety.**

Example:

"What if things don't go as planned?"

"What if I fail?"

"What if I make the wrong decision?"

Reality check:

The future is **unpredictable, no matter how much you try to control it.** Overthinking doesn't **prevent problems**—it just **steals your peace today.** The only way to have a **better future is to be fully present in the now.**

Letting Go of Ego = Letting Go of Unnecessary Stress

The more you **hold onto ego-driven fears,** the less **present, happy, and free** you feel.

But the moment you:

Let go of overanalyzing → You gain **mental clarity.**

Let go of the past → You make room for **growth and peace.**

Let go of future worries → You learn to **trust the process.**

Happiness isn't found in control—it's found in presence.

And the moment you **release ego's grip on your mind,** you unlock **true emotional freedom.**

How to Start Embracing Presence, Intuition, and Inner Peace

The antidote to **ego's chaos?**

Presence. Trust. Flow.

Ego thrives in **attachment**—to the past, to control, to comparison. It pulls you away from **what's real** and keeps you trapped in thoughts that no longer serve you.

But peace? **Peace is found in the present.**

Here's how to step into that energy:

1. Let Go of the Past—It's Already Over

Ego wants you to stay **stuck in the past**—because as long as you're there, you're not moving forward.

It convinces you to:

- **Replay old conversations.**
- **Wish you handled things differently.**
- **Hold onto resentment, shame, or regret.**

But here's the truth:

The past **only has power over you if you keep giving it attention.**

Ask yourself:

Can I change it? → **No? Then let it go.**

Is replaying it helping me? → **No? Then let it go.**

The more you detach from the past, the more peace you create for yourself.

How to stop letting the past control you:

1. Forgive yourself and others—not for them, but for your own peace.

Learn the lesson, but don't relive the pain.

Redirect your focus to what you can create now, not what you wish had happened then.

Letting go doesn't mean **forgetting**—it means you're **choosing peace over attachment.**

2. Stop Trying to Control the Future

Ego craves **certainty.** It wants to **know exactly** how things will go, who will stay, and what will happen.

But the truth?

You can't control everything.

- **You can prepare, but you can't predict.**
- **You can influence, but you can't force.**
- **You can plan, but life will still surprise you.**

Instead of stressing about the future, focus on what you *can* control:

Your mindset → How you choose to see things.

Your energy → What you allow into your space.

Your actions today → The only thing that directly shapes your future.

Trust that everything is unfolding the way it's meant to.

The moment you stop trying to **force outcomes,** you create space for **better ones to come naturally.**

How to release control and embrace trust:

Replace "What if?" thoughts with "Even if, I will be okay." Remind yourself that **uncertainty isn't a threat—it's part of life's flow.**

Know that you are **capable of handling whatever comes next.**

When you **release control, you gain peace.**

3. Stop Letting Ego Distract You From the Present

The present moment is the only place where **life actually happens.**

But ego?

Ego keeps you:

Stuck in the past → Worrying about what you can't change.

Lost in the future → Stressing about what hasn't even happened yet.

If you're **always thinking about what's next, you're missing what's now.**

If you're **always worrying about what already happened, you're wasting the moment you have.**

How to shift into presence:

Breathe. Pay attention to your surroundings.

Slow down. Be fully where you are, not in your head.

Appreciate what's in front of you. Life is happening *now.*

The more **present you are,** the **less power ego has over you.**

Because when you live in **this moment**—fully, completely— you finally experience what it feels like to be **free.**

Exercise: The Ego Release Ritual

To help you identify what your ego is holding onto and consciously let it go to create space for peace, clarity, and freedom.

Step 1: Identify Your Ego Attachments

In a quiet space, take a few deep breaths. Reflect on what's been weighing on your mind. Now, complete these prompts honestly:

- I keep overthinking about...
- I'm holding onto this past situation because...
- I wish I could control...
- I'm afraid of letting go because...

Step 2: What Is Ego Really Trying to Do?

Now go deeper. Ask yourself:

- Is my ego trying to protect me? Impress others? Prove something?
- Is this thought or attachment actually serving me—or stressing me?

Be honest. Write it out.

Step 3: Flip the Script

Now, turn each ego-driven thought into a truth that brings peace.

Example:

"I need to prove I was right" → "I choose peace over being right."

"I can't let go of this mistake" → "I forgive myself and allow growth."

"I'm afraid of what might happen" → "I trust that I'll handle whatever comes."

Write your own ego-to-truth reframe statements now.

Step 4: Release It (For Real)

Pick one thing you're ready to let go of today. Write it down clearly:

"Today, I choose to let go of_____."

Then, say it out loud—or write it on a piece of paper and **rip it up**.

Feel the symbolic power of releasing it. It doesn't control you anymore.

Step 5: Reclaim Your Energy

Now that you've created space, ask yourself:

- What do I want to feel instead?
- What energy or emotion do I choose to replace this with?

Fill in:

"By letting go of_____, I now choose _____."

Example:

By letting go of needing to control everything, I now choose peace and trust.

Reminder:

Letting go is a process. You might need to revisit this ritual more than once—but every time you do, you reclaim a little more of your freedom.

Affirmation:

"I trust myself. I can handle whatever comes."

Final Thoughts: Letting Go = True Power

Ego tells you that **holding on makes you strong.**

That if you just try harder, control more, or prove yourself enough, you'll finally feel secure.

But **real strength?**

Is knowing when to let go.

Is choosing peace over proving a point.

Is embracing flow instead of forcing control.

Letting go isn't **giving up.**

It isn't **losing.**

It isn't **weakness.**

It's the **most powerful thing you can do.**

Because when you let go of:

Ego-driven stress → You gain **clarity.**

Comparison → You gain **self-acceptance.**

Attachment to outcomes → You gain **true freedom.**

You don't **lose anything.**

You gain everything.

Because **freedom, happiness, and clarity** don't come from **holding on.**

They come from **releasing what no longer serves you and stepping fully into the present.**

Chapter 11: Ego vs. Intuition – The Inner Battle

Inside every person, there are **two voices competing for control:**

Ego – Loud, anxious, controlling.

- It speaks in **fear, pride, and insecurity.**
- It makes you **react, doubt, and overanalyze.**
- It thrives on **comparison, validation, and control.**

Intuition – Quiet, wise, calm.

- It speaks in **clarity, deep knowing, and trust.**
- It doesn't force—it **guides.**
- It leads you toward what's **right for you, without fear or pressure.**

Ego keeps you trapped.

Intuition sets you free.

Why Most People Can't Tell the Difference

The biggest challenge? **Ego is louder.**

Ego is fast, intense, and emotionally charged. It drowns out your intuition and convinces you that its voice is the only truth.

Ego reacts. Intuition responds.

Ego is noisy. Intuition is subtle.

Ego is the voice that:

- **Jumps to conclusions** before you have all the facts.
- **Makes decisions out of fear**—fear of missing out, fear of failure, fear of being judged.

- **Overanalyzes everything**, making you second-guess yourself.

Intuition, on the other hand:
- **Feels like a deep knowing**—a calm, unshakable truth.
- **Doesn't rush you.** It whispers, rather than shouts.
- **Doesn't need validation.** It simply knows.

But how do you tell the difference in real-time?

The key is learning to **recognize when ego is speaking—and when intuition is guiding.**

Because once you do?

You unlock a whole new level of **clarity.**

You make decisions that **align with your true self.**

You experience **inner peace instead of inner conflict.**

And that's when life starts to feel **effortless.**

Ego Speaks in Fear—Intuition Speaks in Wisdom

Ego is **rooted in fear.** It operates from **survival instincts**, constantly scanning for danger—even when there is **no real threat.** It's always on edge, anticipating **failure, rejection, or judgment.**

Its job? **To protect you.** But instead of guiding you toward growth, it **keeps you stuck** by making you afraid of taking risks, making changes, or trusting yourself.

Ego says: *"What if you fail? What if they don't like you? What if this goes wrong?"*

Intuition says: *"Even if you fail, you'll learn. Even if they don't like you, you'll be fine. Even if things change, you'll adapt."*

See the difference?

How Ego Keeps You Trapped

Ego operates from scarcity, competition, and insecurity.

- It makes you feel like **you have to prove yourself**—that you're never enough as you are.
- It pushes you to **seek external validation**, convincing you that your worth depends on others' approval.
- It keeps you in **a cycle of fear**, worrying about what could go wrong instead of trusting what could go right.
- It tells you that **change is risky** and that staying where you are—even if you're unhappy—is safer than stepping into the unknown.

Example:

You get a new opportunity → **Ego:** *"What if I'm not ready? What if I fail?"*

You meet someone new → **Ego:** *"What if they don't like me? What if I get hurt?"*

You want to make a change → **Ego:** *"What if this is a mistake? What if I regret it?"*

Ego makes you **fear the worst before it even happens.**

How Intuition Sets You Free

Intuition already knows.

- It doesn't need **proof, reassurance, or validation**—it just *knows.*

154

- It speaks in **calm certainty, not panic or desperation.**
- It guides you through **trust, clarity, and deep inner wisdom.**

Example:

You get a new opportunity → **Intuition:** *"You may not know everything yet, but you'll figure it out."*

You meet someone new → **Intuition:** *"Be present. See where this goes."*

You want to make a change → **Intuition:** *"This feels right. Trust it."*

Intuition doesn't overwhelm you with **what-ifs.** It doesn't create **mental noise.**

It gives you a **subtle but strong knowing**—the kind that doesn't shout, but **feels right in your gut.**

How to Recognize When Your Ego is Drowning Out Your Intuition

One of the biggest reasons people feel **stuck, overwhelmed, or indecisive** is because they **can't tell whether they're listening to ego or intuition.**

Ego is **loud, fearful, and forceful.** It wants you to act **quickly,** out of **pressure, insecurity, or external expectations.**

Intuition is **calm, clear, and steady.** It doesn't rush. It doesn't force. It **guides you with inner knowing, even when it doesn't "make sense" yet.**

If you're struggling to **make a decision** or feeling **stuck,** ask yourself:

Does this voice feel rushed, panicked, or pressured? → That's ego.

Does this voice feel calm, clear, and certain—even if it doesn't "make sense" yet? → That's intuition.

Is this voice feeding my insecurities, comparison, or fear of judgment? → That's ego.

Is this voice guiding me toward what feels right—even if it's uncomfortable? → That's intuition.

Signs Ego is Running the Show

You're making decisions based on fear of failure instead of passion.

If the only reason you're doing (or avoiding) something is **fear of what could go wrong**, ego is in control.

You're overanalyzing and second-guessing everything. Ego **loves** to overthink. It wants to be **100% certain** before making a move—which is impossible.

You feel pressured to prove something instead of just doing what feels right.

Ego constantly asks, *"How will this look?"* instead of *"Does this feel aligned?"*

You keep asking people for validation and approval instead of trusting yourself.

Ego doesn't trust **inner knowing**—it seeks **external confirmation.** If you keep looking for someone to **validate your decision**, ego is in control.

Signs Your Intuition is Speaking

You feel calm and grounded about your decision—even if it's uncertain.

Intuition doesn't need **all the answers**—it just gives you a **sense of peace, even in the unknown.**

You don't need external validation—you just know what's right for you.

When intuition speaks, you don't **obsessively ask for advice**—because deep down, you already *know.*

You feel a deep inner pull toward something, even if your ego doubts it.

It's that **gut feeling** or soft whisper that says, *"This is right for me,"* even when logic says otherwise.

The answer feels natural and aligned, not forced or stressful. Intuition doesn't make you **force things.** It flows, aligns, and feels *right* in a way that ego-driven decisions never do.

The More You Listen to Your Intuition, the Stronger It Gets

Every time you **choose intuition over ego,** you train yourself to:

Trust your inner wisdom instead of seeking external approval.

Make aligned decisions instead of fear-based ones.

Feel peace and clarity instead of stress and overthinking.

The less you let ego control you, the more **freedom, ease, and fulfillment** you'll experience.

Because intuition will **always** lead you where you're meant to go.

The Power of Trusting Your Gut Instead of Ego-Based Thinking

Your **gut instinct—your intuition—is one of your greatest tools.**

It's what leads you to the **right opportunities, the right people, and the right path.** It's an internal compass that **knows what's meant for you**, even before your mind catches up.

But **ego?** Ego will always try to **block it.**

Ego will tell you to stay in a toxic relationship because *"you've already invested too much."*

Ego will make you take a job you hate because *"it looks good on paper."*

Ego will keep you stuck in situations that don't feel right because *"you don't want to fail."*

Ego operates from **fear, pride, and external validation.** Intuition operates from **inner wisdom, trust, and alignment.**

And while **ego argues, justifies, and overthinks—your intuition already knows the truth.**

How to Strengthen Your Intuition

If you feel **disconnected from your gut instinct**, it's because **ego has been drowning it out.** But the good news? **You can always rebuild that connection.**

Quiet the noise.

- Get comfortable with **stillness**—ego needs chaos to thrive, **intuition speaks in silence.**

- Take time to **disconnect** from distractions, social media, and outside opinions.

Stop asking for approval.
- The more you **look outside yourself** for answers, the more you **disconnect from your gut.**
- Trust that **you already have the wisdom you need within you.**

Trust the first feeling.
- **Intuition speaks first—ego overthinks it.**
- That **immediate pull** toward something? Don't dismiss it. It's there for a reason.

Let go of fear-based decisions.
- If **fear is the only reason** you're making a choice, it's ego—not intuition.
- Ask yourself: *"If fear wasn't a factor, what would I choose?"*

The More You Trust Intuition, the Stronger It Gets

Ego makes life complicated. Intuition keeps it simple.

Ego overthinks. Intuition feels.

Ego seeks control. Intuition trusts.

The more you **listen to your gut**, the more **clear, aligned, and confident** your decisions will become.

Because **your intuition will never lead you wrong.**

Exercise: Ego or Intuition? A Self-Check-In

To help you recognize whether you're being guided by ego or intuition in real-time—and strengthen your ability to hear your inner wisdom.

Step 1: Reflect on a Current Decision or Situation

Think of something you're currently struggling with or overthinking.

Write it down:

"The situation I'm trying to figure out is..."

Step 2: Identify the Voice in Your Head

Now listen closely. What are the thoughts coming up? Write them down—*raw, unfiltered, and real.*

"The thoughts in my head sound like..."

Now ask yourself:

- Do these thoughts feel **rushed** or **calm**?
- Do they sound like **fear** or **trust**?
- Do they make me feel **anxious** or **at peace**?

Use this quick cheat sheet:

If it sounds like...	It's probably...
"What if I mess up?"	Ego
"This just feels right, even if it's scary."	Intuition
"What will they think of me?"	Ego
"I know this is meant for me."	Intuition
"I have to prove myself."	Ego

If it sounds like...	It's probably...
"I don't need proof. I just know."	Intuition

Which voice is leading you right now?
Ego or Intuition ?

Step 3: Ask the Grounding Question

This one question can shift everything: *"If fear wasn't part of the equation, what would I choose?"*

Write your answer with full honesty.

"Without fear, I would..."

Step 4: Choose Your Guide

Now it's time to consciously choose who's in charge.

"I choose to listen to _____ because _____." (Example: *"I choose to listen to my intuition because it leads me to peace, not pressure."*)

The more you pause to check in, the louder your intuition becomes. Ego reacts. Intuition responds. Your clarity lives in stillness—*go there often.*

Final Thoughts: Choose Intuition Over Ego, and Life Gets Easier

Ego makes life **complicated.** It makes you **chase, doubt, and prove.**

It keeps you **second-guessing** your path, fearing failure, and seeking approval.

But **intuition?**

It simplifies. No overthinking—just clarity.

It brings peace. No unnecessary stress—just trust.

It aligns you with what's truly right for you. No forcing—just flow.

The moment you stop letting **ego drown out your intuition,** everything shifts:

You make better decisions. Choices feel *aligned*, not pressured.

You stop needing validation. You trust *yourself* first.

You move toward the life you're actually meant for. The *right* people, places, and opportunities begin to unfold naturally.

Because when **intuition leads,** life doesn't feel like a struggle— it feels like alignment.

Chapter 12: The Strength in Humility

Most people think confidence means:

Being the loudest in the room.

Having all the answers.

Making sure everyone knows how great you are.

But **real confidence?**

Comes from mastery, not from proving yourself.

Comes from humility, not from ego.

Comes from knowing who you are so deeply that you don't need to prove anything to anyone.

The strongest people **aren't the ones demanding attention—** they're the ones who **don't need it.**

They don't need to:

Constantly remind people of their worth.

Seek validation through dominance or superiority.

Win every argument just to be "right."

Because when you **truly understand yourself, your worth, and your abilities**, you no longer have to **fight for recognition.**

You **just embody it.**

And **that's why humility is a superpower.**

How Real Self-Confidence Comes from Mastery, Not Proving Yourself

Ego **wants to prove something.**

It craves:

Validation → Needing others to recognize your worth.

Competition → Trying to be better than everyone else.

Recognition → Seeking attention to feel important.

But **real confidence?**

It comes from **knowing.**

It comes from **mastery.**

It comes from **internal certainty, not external validation.**

A **true master** doesn't need to tell people they're great—**they just are.**

A **skilled artist** doesn't need to say, *"I'm talented."* **Their work speaks for itself.**

A **true leader** doesn't have to scream, *"I'm in charge."* **Their energy makes people follow.**

A **deeply wise person** doesn't argue to prove they're right—**they listen, observe, and respond with clarity.**

When you **know who you are and what you're capable of,** you stop wasting energy **trying to prove it to people who don't matter.**

Mastery vs. Ego-Based Confidence

Ego-Based Confidence → *"I need people to see how good I am."*

Mastery-Based Confidence → *"I know I'm good, whether people see it or not."*

Ego-Based Confidence → *"I need to win arguments to prove I'm right."*

Mastery-Based Confidence → *"I don't need to convince people— I let my actions speak."*

Ego-Based Confidence → *"I have to be better than everyone else."*

Mastery-Based Confidence → *"I focus on being better than I was yesterday."*

Instead of This → Shift to This

Seeking approval → Trusting yourself.

Competing with others → Mastering your own path.

Defending yourself → Letting your results speak for you.

Because **real confidence isn't about making noise**—it's about quietly becoming **so good that you no longer need validation.**

Why Humility is a Superpower—How Staying Grounded Keeps You Ahead

The world **rewards confidence,** but it **respects humility.**

Humility isn't about **downplaying yourself**—it's about staying **grounded** so you can **keep growing.**

The strongest, most successful people aren't the ones **constantly proving their greatness**—they're the ones **who remain teachable, adaptable, and self-aware.**

Here's why **humility keeps you ahead:**

It keeps you open to learning.

- **Ego thinks it already knows everything.**
- **Humility knows there's always more to learn.**
- The moment you believe you have nothing left to learn, you stop evolving.

It attracts the right people.

- People trust and respect those who are **confident but not arrogant.**
- Humility makes you **approachable, relatable, and respected.**

165

- No one likes working with someone who always **acts like they're the smartest in the room.**

It helps you handle success with grace.
- The higher you rise, the more **ego wants to take over.**
- Humility keeps you **centered, focused, and grateful.**
- It reminds you that success isn't just about **status—it's about impact.**

It allows you to let go of mistakes without shame.
- When you're humble, you don't take **failure personally**—you take it **as a lesson.**
- Instead of **defending your mistakes**, you **own them, learn, and move forward.**

The Power of Humility: You Stop Needing to Prove Yourself

The moment you stop **seeking approval, competing for attention, or trying to prove your worth**—you gain something even better:

Effortless respect.

Genuine influence.

A mindset built for long-term success.

Because **true strength isn't about proving your greatness—** it's about constantly improving it.

Signs You're Overcoming Ego and Growing Into Your Best Self

So how do you know you're **breaking free from ego** and stepping into your **highest self?**

It's not about **perfection**—it's about **awareness and growth.**

Here's how you'll know you're leveling up:

1. You Stop Taking Everything Personally

Ego makes everything about you. Growth helps you realize **most things aren't personal.**

Someone criticizes you? → *You listen, take what's useful, and keep moving.*

Someone doesn't like you? → *You don't need their approval to validate your worth.*

Someone succeeds? → *You celebrate them instead of feeling like you're falling behind.*

The more secure you are, the less reactive you become.

2. You Value Growth Over Being Right

Ego needs to be right. Growth prioritizes **learning, evolving, and understanding.**

You don't need to **win arguments**—you'd rather **understand.** You don't feel **threatened by new perspectives**—you embrace them.
You don't resist **feedback**—you use it to **get better.**

When growth becomes more important than ego, every experience becomes a lesson.

3. You No Longer Chase Validation

Ego constantly seeks approval. Growth teaches you to **validate yourself.**

You do things because they **feel right**, not because they **look good.**

You trust your **intuition** instead of seeking **constant reassurance.**

You focus on **personal fulfillment**, not just **external applause.**

The more you approve of yourself, the less you need approval from others.

4. You Move with Quiet Confidence

Ego needs to prove itself. True confidence is **felt, not forced.**

You no longer feel the need to **prove yourself in every conversation.**

You don't feel **jealous when others win**—you know your time is coming.

You trust your **skills, effort, and purpose**—and you let your results **speak for themselves.**

When you stop trying to be seen as great and just focus on being great, everything shifts.

5. You Feel Peace Instead of Pressure

Ego makes life feel like a competition. Growth allows you to **flow with life, not fight it.**

You stop **forcing things that aren't meant for you.**

You stop **needing to control everything.**

You stop **living for external success** and start **living for inner peace.**

That's when you know you've truly mastered ego.

Because the goal **was never to destroy ego—it was to rise above it.**

Less proving. More being. More peace.

Exercise: Humble Confidence Check-In

To help you recognize where ego might be driving your need to prove yourself—and guide you back to a grounded, powerful, humble version of confidence.

Step 1: Where Are You Trying to Prove Something?

Think of an area in your life where you feel pressure to prove yourself or be seen a certain way.

"Lately, I feel like I need to prove myself in..." (e.g., work, social media, relationships, etc.)

Now ask yourself:

- What am I trying to prove?
- Who am I trying to prove it to?
- What do I hope to gain from being seen a certain way?

Write it out, no filter.

Step 2: Is This Ego or Mastery Talking?

Reflect on your intentions behind your actions.

For each statement below, check which voice is leading you:

"I need to win this argument to be respected."

"I trust my work speaks for itself."

"I feel jealous when others succeed."

"I'm focused on being better than I was yesterday."

"I need people to see how talented I am."

"I do this because I love it, not for approval."

Notice any patterns? Where is your ego trying to steal the spotlight?

Step 3: Reclaim Quiet Power

Now, shift the energy. Fill in the blank below:

"I don't need to prove _____ because I already know _____."

Example: *"I don't need to prove I'm smart because I already know I'm capable and always learning."*

Step 4: Ground Yourself in Growth

Answer this:

"If I were operating from humility and inner strength, I would..."

(What would you do differently today? Speak less? Listen more? Trust yourself more?)

Step 5: Lock It In with a Grounding Mantra

Choose one or write your own:

- **"I let my work speak for itself."**
- **"I don't compete—I improve."**
- **"Real power is quiet."**

Say it aloud. Breathe it in. Move with it.

Final Thoughts: Mastering Ego is the Ultimate Power Move

Ego makes you **loud, reactive, and insecure.** Mastery makes you **calm, collected, and unstoppable.**

And the real flex? **Is not needing to flex at all.**

The most **powerful** people in the world?

They don't waste energy **proving themselves.**

They don't seek **external validation.**

They don't let **ego control their emotions, decisions, or path.**

They just **live in alignment, trust themselves, and let their actions do the talking.**

And now, **you're stepping into that version of yourself.**

Because once you **transcend ego,** you don't just win—

You rise above the need to compete at all.

Chapter 13: Ego and Overachievement – The Toxic Hustle

Hustle culture loves to dress up ego as ambition.

Work harder. Sleep less. Grind nonstop. Be "booked and busy." Keep achieving. Keep proving. Keep performing.

But here's the truth nobody wants to say:

Sometimes ambition isn't drive — it's desperation.

Not for success... but for validation.

Not for growth... but for *proof* that you're finally enough.

When your ego gets attached to overachievement, productivity becomes your personality. Your value becomes measured in output. And rest? Rest feels like failure.

You don't know how to stop. You *can't* stop. Because slowing down means facing the question your ego is terrified of:

"Who am I without my achievements?"

When Ambition Becomes Identity

There's nothing wrong with wanting more for yourself.

Dream big. Work hard. Go after the life you deserve.

But the moment "more" becomes your definition of *who you are*, your ambition stops being a tool — and starts being a trap.

Because ego?

Ego doesn't want growth. Ego wants glory.

It feeds off applause. Off recognition. Off the illusion that *being seen as successful* equals *being enough*.

And every time you get that next win — the raise, the degree, the praise, the follower count, the compliment — you feel a rush.

But it doesn't last. It never does. Because the ego's hunger is bottomless.

That high? It's temporary. So you chase the next hit. And then the next.

You build your life like a résumé — a checklist of proof that you matter.

Your schedule becomes your self-worth. Your to-do list becomes your lifeline. You confuse productivity with purpose.

Before you know it, you're not just chasing goals — you *are* the chase.

You're not just achieving — you're *performing worthiness* on loop.

And when the performance stops? When life throws you a curveball, or you finally sit still for five minutes? The ego panics.

Because without the constant "doing," it doesn't know *who you are*.

- If you don't hit that deadline, are you still disciplined?
- If you take a break, are you still valuable?
- If you stop producing, are you still *enough*?

That's when the shame creeps in. The guilt. The fear of falling behind. The identity crisis.

Because you've tied your existence to your output. You've made success your oxygen.

But real talk?

That's not ambition. That's addiction — to external validation.

That's not drive.

173

That's ego in a burnout disguise, whispering that your worth is conditional.

And here's the truth: anything conditional is fragile. When your worth is based on constant achievement, it only takes one failure — or one season of stillness — to make it all collapse.

You weren't born to chase worth.

You were born with it.

Let ambition be the engine, not the identity.

Because you're not here just to *achieve* your life — you're here to *live* it.

That's ego in a burnout disguise.

The Cost of Constant Hustle

Let's be real: **overachievement is often a trauma response dressed up as ambition.**

It's the ego's way of trying to control the chaos — to guarantee safety by becoming *so good, so successful, so impressive* that nothing bad can touch you.

It's not just about winning — it's about *surviving*.

But here's the truth: all that constant proving? It comes with a price.

Chronic Stress and Anxiety

Your nervous system is in go-mode 24/7. Even when your body's still, your mind is racing — planning, overthinking, strategizing, worrying. You can't relax because your self-worth feels tied to how much you've "accomplished" that day. Peace feels unfamiliar. Stillness feels unsafe.

Never Feeling Truly Present

You're always in the next moment. The next task. The next goal. Even when you're with people you love, part of you is somewhere else — mentally checking off boxes, thinking about what hasn't been done, or calculating your next move. You're there, but not *there*.

Relationships That Suffer

When you're consumed with overachieving, you don't have much left to give emotionally. Friends, partners, family — they start to feel your absence, even when you're physically present. You're always busy, always distracted, always "just trying to get this one thing done." Eventually, connection starts to fade.

Guilt When You're Not Being "Productive"

Even your rest turns into a performance. You feel lazy for sleeping in. You can't enjoy a day off without feeling like you're falling behind. The guilt eats away at you — because somewhere deep down, your ego convinced you that **you have to earn rest.**

But let's be clear:

Rest isn't a reward. Rest is your *right*.

You don't have to exhaust yourself to justify existing. You don't have to push yourself to the edge just to prove you deserve love, success, or peace.

You are not a machine. You are not your productivity. You are a human being who is allowed to *pause, breathe,* and *just be.*

Burnout is not a badge of honor.

Being constantly overwhelmed is not a flex.

And living in a cycle of hustle and collapse isn't sustainable —
it's self-abandonment.

Rebuilding Your Worth Outside of Productivity

Healing from hustle culture isn't about giving up on your goals.
It's about *reclaiming yourself* from the idea that you only matter
when you're producing something.

Your worth was never meant to be earned — it was always
meant to be honored.

So if you've been defining yourself by your deadlines, your
output, your status, or your success... it's time to come back home to
you.

Here's what healing looks like — not just in theory, but in
practice:

1. Detach Your Identity from Your Achievements

Start with this question:

Who am I when I'm not working, achieving, or striving?
If the silence after that question makes you uncomfortable — that's
where the work begins.

Because your identity isn't your job title.

It's not your hustle, your GPA, your business, or your bank
account.

You're allowed to exist without performing.

You're allowed to be proud of yourself even on your
"unproductive" days.

You're allowed to breathe without building something every
second.

Your value isn't based on how much you do — it's based on *who you are when there's nothing left to prove.*

2. Rest Without Guilt

You don't need to earn your rest. You don't need to justify it. You don't need to schedule it *only* after you've pushed yourself to the point of exhaustion.

Rest is not weakness. It's wisdom.

It's you choosing sustainability over self-destruction.

It's how you make space for clarity, creativity, and longevity.

Your ego will tell you rest is lazy.

That you're falling behind. That someone else is working harder.

But real power isn't found in pushing nonstop — it's found in knowing *when to pause, when to recharge,* and *when to say, "I matter more than my checklist."*

3. Choose Presence Over Performance

You don't have to constantly impress. You don't have to prove your growth by turning your healing into content or your goals into a performance.

What if *this moment* was enough?

What if your current peace was more powerful than your next milestone?

Choose to be here. Right now. In your body. In your breath. In your life.

Don't just *document* the journey — *live* it.

4. Celebrate Being, Not Just Doing

You are not a machine. You were not put here just to hustle, strive, and collapse.

You are here to feel. To grow. To love. To rest. To laugh. To connect. To evolve.

You don't need to reach a certain level to deserve joy. You don't need to accomplish something to feel proud.

Being *you* — with presence, intention, and compassion — is already a success.

So celebrate yourself for the moments no one sees. The quiet growth. The inner work. The boundaries. The healing. The *being*.

Because that? That's where your real worth lives.

When Success Becomes a Distraction from Self

One of ego's sneakiest tricks is convincing you that success will heal what only self-connection can.

You start chasing more, not because you're ungrateful—but because you're disconnected. Because somewhere deep down, you're hoping that if you just achieve enough, it'll silence the voice inside that says you're not enough yet.

But no level of success can fill the space where your soul is asking for your presence.

You'll keep stacking accomplishments and still feel empty. You'll hit milestone after milestone and still wonder why you don't feel fulfilled. Because ego wants you to be busy—not self-aware. It wants noise, not stillness. Movement, not mindfulness.

And when you never pause long enough to meet yourself underneath the hustle, you start mistaking success for self.

But real growth? Real peace? Real power? It's in the pause. It's in learning how to exist without performance. It's in letting yourself be still and whole at the same time.

You are not falling behind. You are not lazy for needing a break. You are not weak for wanting a life that feels good, not just looks good.

You're healing. You're shedding the layers of ego that taught you love must be earned and worth must be proven.

You are not the hustle. You are the heart behind it.

Reflective Exercise: Who Am I Without the Hustle?

This isn't about abandoning your goals — it's about *separating your worth* from your work.

Take a few minutes, get still, and answer honestly:

1. **What makes me feel valuable — and why?**
   (Is it accomplishments? Productivity? Being seen as "driven"?)

2. **When I'm not actively achieving something, how do I feel?**
   (Restless? Guilty? Lost? Free?)

3. **What would it look like to feel proud of myself... just for *being* me?**
   (No projects. No to-do list. Just presence.)

4. **What parts of me have I been neglecting in the name of "grind mode"?**
   (Creativity, relationships, rest, joy, health, fun?)

5. **If I took a break today, what fear would come up —
   and is it even true?**

This isn't about quitting.

This is about *reclaiming yourself from the identity of performance*.

You're allowed to thrive *without* burning out.

Affirmation Drop

- *"I am worthy, even when I'm resting."*
- *"My existence is not a project to be managed — it is a life to be lived."*

Ambition is beautiful — until it becomes a prison.
True success is being at peace with yourself, not just busy with your goals.

When you let go of the need to *prove* your worth, you finally get to *live* your life.

Part 4: Ego & Success – The Silent Killer of Potential

Ego doesn't just affect your emotions and relationships—it can also **sabotage your success.**

Most people think ego is what drives ambition. They believe confidence, risk-taking, and power come from having a strong ego.

But in reality?

Ego makes people **arrogant instead of skilled.**

Ego makes people **seek attention instead of mastery.**

Ego makes people **chase short-term validation instead of long-term growth.**

The biggest mistake successful people make? **Thinking they're above learning, improving, or adapting.** That's when ego **kills potential.**

If you want real, lasting success—not just surface-level wins— **you need to master ego before it masters you.**

Chapter 14: When Ego Makes You Your Own Worst Enemy

Ego is the ultimate trickster.

It makes you believe that **your success is all your doing** and that **your failures are someone else's fault.**

It convinces you that **you already know everything**—so you stop learning.

It makes you **crave being the smartest person in the room**—so you stop growing.

And before you know it, **you're the reason you're not progressing.**

Ego makes you **fight battles that don't need to be fought, burn bridges that should be crossed, and reject lessons that could change your life.**

If you don't recognize when your ego is sabotaging you, **you'll keep tripping over your own feet—without even realizing you're the one who put obstacles in your path.**

How Ego Makes You Misinterpret Success and Failure

Ego loves **rewriting the story** to make you look like the hero—whether it's claiming full credit for success or shifting all blame when things go wrong.

It creates **two major illusions:**

1. "I did this all by myself" → The lie of over crediting success

2. "It's not my fault" → The lie of avoiding responsibility

Both of these mindsets keep you **stuck in self-deception**, preventing real growth.

Ego's Favorite Lie: "I Did This All By Myself"

When things go well, ego wants **all the credit.**

Got a promotion? → *"It's because I'm the best."*

Closed a big deal? → *"I did that all on my own."*

Hit a major goal? → *"It's because I'm better than the rest."*

But here's the **truth:**

Your hard work matters—but so do external factors.

- The **opportunities** you were given.
- The **people** who supported or guided you.
- The **luck, timing, or circumstances** that played a role.

Ego **hates admitting this** because it wants to believe *you* are the sole reason for your success.

 The danger? If you think success is all yours, you'll **underestimate the effort it takes to stay successful.**

You'll stop **learning, improving, and adapting**—because you think you've "made it."

You'll start **looking down on others**, assuming they just "aren't working as hard" instead of recognizing the complex factors that contribute to success.

Real winners stay grateful, self-aware, and humble enough to keep improving.

They recognize that **success is a mix of effort, opportunity, and adaptability.**

Ego's Second Favorite Lie: "It's Not My Fault"

When things go **wrong**, ego refuses to take responsibility.

Lost a job? → *"They didn't appreciate me."*

Relationship failed? → *"They were the problem."*

Business mistake? → *"The market wasn't fair."*

Ego makes you **blame external factors** instead of **looking inward.**

Instead of asking, *"What could I have done differently?"*, ego says, *"That wasn't my fault."*

Instead of owning up to mistakes, ego **finds excuses and scapegoats.**

Instead of growing, ego **keeps you stuck in the same cycles.**

The problem? If you never take responsibility, you **never grow.** If everything is **always someone else's fault,** you **never improve.** If you always play **the victim,** you give away your **power to change your situation.**

Successful people don't waste time making excuses. They:

Own their mistakes.

Learn from their failures.

Make adjustments and keep moving.

Because **growth only happens when you take accountability.**

Ego wants to **protect your pride.**

But your **higher self wants to evolve.**

The choice? **Stay stuck in illusions or step into real growth.**

Thinking You Know Everything Instead of Staying Open to Learning

Ego hates being challenged. It hates being wrong. It hates admitting there's more to learn. That's why some of the most talented, intelligent, and capable people stop growing—not because they lack ability, but because they stop being open to growth.

Instead of pushing themselves to improve, they start believing:

- "I've already mastered this."
- "I don't need feedback—I know what I'm doing."
- "No one can teach me anything I don't already know."

This mindset creates an invisible ceiling. It keeps people stuck, no matter how much potential they have. They might continue doing what they're good at, but they won't reach their highest level because they've already decided they have nothing left to learn.

The irony? True masters never stop learning. The best in any field—from athletes to entrepreneurs, artists to scientists—actively seek growth. They welcome new perspectives, challenge their own beliefs, and understand that mastery is an ongoing process, not a final destination.

The moment you believe you know everything is the moment you stop evolving.

Growth comes from humility—the ability to say, "I don't know everything, but I'm willing to learn." It comes from recognizing that knowledge is infinite, and no matter how much you've achieved, there's always room to improve.

The difference between those who plateau and those who continue rising is simple: **curiosity.**

- Be curious about what you don't know.
- Be willing to challenge your own thinking.
- Be open to learning from anyone—even those you least expect.

Because the people who stay students, keep winning.

The Addiction to Being the Smartest Person in the Room

Ego loves feeling superior. It thrives on being the one with all the answers, the one people turn to for guidance, the one who seems to have it all figured out. But that craving for intellectual dominance comes at a cost—stagnation.

Here's the danger in always needing to be the smartest person in the room:

If you're always the smartest person in the room, you're in the wrong room.

When you're constantly the most knowledgeable, there's no one to push you further. You might feel accomplished, but you're not evolving.

If no one challenges you, you're not growing.

Growth happens when your ideas are questioned, when you're forced to think deeper, when someone else's perspective stretches your mind. Surrounding yourself with people who only affirm your intelligence keeps you comfortable—but comfort doesn't create progress.

If you always feel like the best, you're probably surrounded by people who won't push you higher.

The strongest, most successful people aren't afraid to put themselves in rooms where they *aren't* the best. They seek out mentors, experts, and competitors who challenge them. They embrace feeling out of their depth because they know that's where real growth happens.

The smartest move isn't proving you're the best—it's putting yourself in spaces where you can *become* better.

Instead of chasing superiority, chase **growth.**

- Be willing to be the least experienced person in the room.
- Surround yourself with people who inspire you to level up.
- Seek out conversations that challenge your perspective.

The moment you stop feeding your ego and start feeding your mind, everything changes.

Exercise: Mirror Check – Is Ego Holding You Back?

To identify where ego might be sabotaging your growth, blocking your success, or distorting your perspective—and begin shifting toward humility, accountability, and real growth.

Step 1: Spot the Ego Patterns

Answer the following honestly. Don't judge—just observe.

When something goes wrong, my first thought is usually...

    (a) "Whose fault is this?"

    (b) "What did I miss?"

    (c) "How can I avoid this next time?"

When I succeed, I usually think...

    (a) "I did that all by myself."

    (b) "I worked hard, but I had support."

    (c) "I'm grateful for the timing, help, and growth."

When someone challenges my ideas or opinions, I...

    (a) Get defensive or annoyed.

    (b) Listen, but still feel like I need to prove I'm right.

    (c) Stay curious and open to other perspectives.

When I'm the smartest person in the room, I feel...

    (a) Superior.

    (b) Comfortable.

    (c) Bored—and ready to find a new room.

Count how many "a," "b," and "c" answers you have. More "a"s? Ego's running the show. More "c"s? You're leading with growth.

Step 2: Identify One Area Where Ego Might Be Holding You Back

What's one area of your life where you've been blaming others, refusing feedback, or feeling like you already know it all?

Write it out clearly:

"Lately, my ego has been showing up in _____ by _____."

(Example: *"Lately, my ego has been showing up in my job by resisting feedback and thinking I'm always right."*)

Step 3: Flip the Script

Now shift from ego to growth with this reframe:

"Instead of _____, I choose to _____."

(Example: *"Instead of resisting feedback, I choose to stay open and learn from it."*)

"I'm not too good for _____. I'm always a student."

(Example: *"I'm not too good for mentorship or correction. I'm always a student."*)

Step 4: Do a Humility Audit

Write down 3 things that contributed to your success that had *nothing to do with you* (support, timing, luck, mentors, environment, etc.)

Now write 1 mistake or failure you've been blaming on someone else—and **take ownership** of the role you played:

"I've been blaming _____ for _____, but my role in it was _____."

Step 5: Commit to Being Challenged

Where can you intentionally place yourself in a room where you're not the most knowledgeable?

(Think: mentorship, feedback sessions, mastermind groups, tough conversations.)

Write your next step:

"To grow, I will challenge myself by _____."

Final Grounding Statement:

"My ego doesn't define me—my willingness to grow does."

Final Thoughts: Ego Can Be Your Biggest Enemy—Or Your Greatest Teacher

Ego isn't just something that affects relationships or emotions—it can be the biggest roadblock to your success. It can blind you to your weaknesses, keep you stuck in your comfort zone, and make you resistant to change. But here's the good news: **you control it.**

Ego doesn't have to be your downfall—it can be your teacher. It can show you where you need to grow, where you're holding yourself back, and where you need to humble yourself to move forward. The key is learning how to manage it.

Take credit for your work—but also recognize the luck, timing, and people who helped you.

Confidence and gratitude can coexist. Acknowledge your hard work, but don't let ego trick you into thinking you did it *all* alone.

Own your mistakes instead of making excuses. The strongest people take accountability. They don't shift blame, justify bad decisions, or let pride get in the way of growth.

Stay open to learning, no matter how much you already know.
No matter how skilled, intelligent, or accomplished you become, there's always more to learn. The moment you think you've "arrived" is the moment you stop growing.

Surround yourself with people who challenge you, not just people who praise you.
Growth doesn't happen in echo chambers. It happens in rooms where you're pushed, questioned, and encouraged to level up.

At the end of the day, **ego can either hold you back—or fuel your growth.** It can make you defensive, stagnant, and blind to opportunities, or it can be the mirror that helps you see where you need to improve.

The choice is yours.

Chapter 15: How People Use Your Ego to Keep You Small

Not everyone wants to see you win. And the most dangerous obstacles to your success aren't always outright enemies or obvious haters—they're often the people who smile in your face while subtly keeping you stuck.

They may not even do it out of malice. Sometimes, it's their own insecurities speaking. **Your growth forces them to confront their own lack of progress.** Your ambition makes them feel insecure about their own stagnation. Your willingness to evolve makes them afraid of being left behind. And instead of rising with you, they'd rather keep you where they feel comfortable.

And the easiest way to keep you small? **Playing with your ego.**

Some people will manipulate your confidence, not by tearing you down directly, but by subtly influencing the way you think about yourself:

Some will gas you up at the wrong times. They'll hype up your bad decisions, stroke your ego when you should be reflecting, and encourage impulsive moves that lead to self-sabotage. They don't want you to truly succeed—they just want you to feel invincible enough to crash.

Some will discourage you subtly. Instead of outright saying, "You can't do this," they'll plant little seeds of doubt. "Are you sure this is a good idea?" "That sounds risky." "I don't know if people like us really succeed in things like that." Over time, those whispers become your own internal voice, keeping you stuck in fear.

Some will disguise fear as advice. They'll act like they're looking out for you, but really, they're projecting their own insecurities. "I just don't want you to get your hopes up." "Maybe you should wait until the timing is better." "I wouldn't do that if I were you." They aren't protecting you—they're keeping you from taking the risks necessary to grow.

The more you succeed, the more you'll recognize these patterns. And the key to rising above? **Knowing when your ego is being used against you.**

Because once you see the game, you can stop playing it.

Why Some People Don't Want You to Succeed

Success is a mirror. It reflects back not just your achievements but also the choices and limitations of those around you.

When you grow, it reflects back to others what they aren't doing.

Some people are comfortable where they are. They've made peace with their own stagnation. But when they see you striving for more—taking risks, making moves, leveling up—it forces them to confront the reality that they *could* be doing the same. And that realization can be uncomfortable.

When you change, it forces them to question if they should change too.

Growth challenges the status quo. It disrupts the unspoken agreements people have about who they are and what they're capable of. If you break out of your box, it forces them to ask: *What's stopping me from doing the same?* Some people will embrace that challenge. Others will resent it.

When you step into your power, it threatens those who rely on your old self.

Not everyone in your life benefits from your success. Some people were comfortable with the version of you that played small, that settled, that didn't make waves. If they depended on you to stay the same—whether for their own validation, security, or sense of control—your growth feels like a loss to them.

That's why some people will:

Minimize your accomplishments.

"It's not that impressive." "Anyone could've done that." They'll downplay your success so you don't feel like it's worth celebrating. If they admit you've achieved something meaningful, they have to acknowledge what they *haven't* achieved.

Downplay your dreams.

"That sounds unrealistic." "Are you sure you want to risk that?" They'll cast doubt on your aspirations, not because they truly think you'll fail, but because *your willingness to try* makes them feel inadequate for not trying themselves.

Remind you of your past failures.

"Remember the last time you tried this?" "Didn't you already fail at something like this before?" Instead of supporting your growth, they weaponize your past against you, as if past mistakes define your future.

Make you feel like you're abandoning them.

"You're changing too much." "You're not the same person anymore." This is one of the most manipulative tactics, making you feel guilty for evolving. In reality, you're not leaving them behind—they're just unwilling to grow alongside you.

But here's the truth:

Your growth doesn't make them shrink. It doesn't take anything away from them. Their reaction isn't about you—it's about their own fears, doubts, and insecurities. And if you're not careful, their words can become your inner voice, making you second-guess yourself and hesitate when you should be moving forward.

The key is to recognize these patterns and remind yourself: **You are not responsible for their discomfort.** Your only responsibility is to keep growing, keep pushing, and keep becoming the version of yourself that you're meant to be.

How People Will Discourage You to Keep You in the Same Place

Not all discouragement is obvious. It's not always loud, aggressive, or openly negative. Sometimes, it's subtle—wrapped in the illusion of concern, disguised as advice, or hidden in the words of people who claim to have your best interests at heart.

Some people won't straight-up say, *"I don't want you to succeed."* Instead, they'll plant tiny seeds of doubt, hoping they take root and make you second-guess yourself. And if you're not paying attention, their words can slowly chip away at your confidence, convincing you to stay exactly where you are.

Common Tactics People Use to Keep You Small

Doubt disguised as concern – "Are you sure you're ready for that?"

At first, it sounds like they're just looking out for you. But what they're really doing is making you question your own readiness. The truth is, *no one* feels 100% ready before they take a big step. Growth happens in the doing, not the waiting.

Guilt-tripping your growth – "You've changed... you used to be more fun."

Translation: *I liked you better when you weren't prioritizing yourself.* When people feel threatened by your growth, they'll try to make you feel guilty for evolving. But growing doesn't mean you're abandoning them—it just means you're stepping into the person you were always meant to be.

Bringing up old failures – "Remember when you tried something similar and it didn't work?"

Your past mistakes become their favorite weapon. They act like your failures define you, when in reality, every successful person has failed multiple times. What they don't realize is, *every time you fail, you learn. And every time you learn, you get closer to success.*

Comparing you to others – "There are already so many people doing that—why would anyone pick you?"

They'll make you feel like there's no space for you, like you have nothing unique to offer. But the truth is, **no one can do it exactly like you.** Your perspective, your style, your voice—that's what makes it different.

Over-exaggerating the risks – "You could lose everything."

They'll paint the worst-case scenario as if it's the only possible outcome. Yes, risk exists. But so does *reward.* Every success story starts with someone who was willing to take a chance.

Why They Do It

Some of them **genuinely believe** they're helping you. They project their own fears onto you, thinking they're keeping you safe. Others just **don't want to feel left behind.** Your growth forces them to face their own lack of progress, and instead of rising with you, they try to hold you back.

Either way, their words can become **the chains that hold you back—if you let them.**

But here's the truth: Their fears don't have to be yours. Their limitations don't have to define you. The only way to break free is to recognize the patterns, trust yourself, and keep moving forward—no matter what they say.

How to Differentiate Real Advice from Ego-Based Sabotage

Not all criticism is bad. Some advice is **valuable, necessary, and worth listening to.** Some warnings are real and can help you avoid major pitfalls. The challenge is **knowing who to listen to**—because not everyone giving advice actually wants to see you win.

Some people offer **wisdom.** Others project **fear, doubt, and insecurity.** The key is knowing the difference.

How to Tell If Advice Is Coming from Wisdom or Insecurity
Real Advice:

Comes from people who have *done* what you're trying to do. They've walked the path, made mistakes, learned lessons, and have insights that can genuinely help you.

Is **balanced**—they acknowledge risks but also offer solutions. They don't just tell you what *could* go wrong; they also tell you how to make it *go right.*

Encourages growth, not limitation. Real mentors push you forward. They don't tell you to shrink—they tell you how to expand wisely.

Ego-Based Sabotage:

Comes from people who have **never taken risks themselves.** They don't have firsthand experience, just opinions based on fear.

Uses **fear to hold you back** instead of guiding you forward. Instead of helping you prepare, they just make you doubt yourself.

Feels **more about their doubts than your actual potential.** It's not about whether you *can* succeed—it's about the fact that *they* never tried, so they assume you won't either.

Test This: The "Who Is Talking?" Check

Before letting someone's words affect your confidence, **pause and ask yourself:**

Are they living the life I want?

If they aren't where I want to be, why would their opinion shape my path? Would I trade places with them? If not, I shouldn't let their mindset influence mine.

Are they projecting their own fears onto me?

People often criticize what they're too afraid to do themselves. If someone has never taken a leap of faith, they might try to convince you it's impossible—because *they* never had the courage to try.

Is this advice limiting me or pushing me toward growth?

Real guidance helps you move forward. If the advice is making you feel smaller, more doubtful, or hesitant for no real reason, it's not advice—it's projection.

At the end of the day, **the only opinions that should shape your path are from those who truly understand the journey.** Choose your mentors wisely, trust your own instincts, and never let someone else's fear become your limitation.

Why I Don't Listen to Anyone Who Isn't Where I Want to Be

I don't take advice from people who aren't living the life I want. Period. Even if what they're saying *sounds* like good advice, I still don't listen—because sometimes, what sounds logical or reasonable is actually just a reflection of **their own limitations, not mine.**

At the end of the day, advice is only as valuable as the person giving it. **If they knew better, they would do better.**

That's why I only take advice from people who have *actually succeeded* at what I'm trying to accomplish. Not people who think they know. Not people who *could have* made it but didn't. Not people who have an opinion but no results to back it up.

Because here's the truth:

Most people give advice based on what they think is possible for themselves. If they believe success is unlikely for them, they'll assume the same for you. If they've failed, they might assume failure is inevitable.

Some advice sounds good but keeps you small. Just because advice *makes sense* doesn't mean it's right. Some people will tell you to "be realistic" when being realistic is what keeps them stuck. Some will warn you about risks, but only because they were too scared to take them.

What you want vs. what you need. Sometimes, what people tell you sounds like what you *need* to hear, but in reality, it's just what keeps you comfortable. I don't let advice steer me toward what's "safe" if it means sacrificing what I actually *want* in life.

If they haven't done it, how can they teach it? It's simple: You wouldn't take fitness advice from someone who's out of shape. You wouldn't take financial advice from someone who's broke. So why take life advice from someone who hasn't achieved what you're working toward?

Listen to winners. Listen to doers. Listen to people who have already walked the path. Because anyone who *really* knows what it takes to succeed will never discourage you from going after it.

Exercise: Reclaiming Your Power — Who's Really In Your Ear?

To help you identify whose voices have been shaping your self-belief, recognize if those voices are rooted in fear or growth, and start trusting yourself over other people's insecurities.

Step 1: Who's Influencing You Right Now?

Think of 2–3 people whose opinions or advice have *seriously affected* your confidence or direction lately.

Next to each name, write a recent thing they said that stuck with you (good or bad):

Example: *"Maybe you should wait until you're more ready."*

Step 2: Ask the "WHO IS TALKING?" Questions

Now go through each person and ask:

- Have they done what I'm trying to do?
- Are they living the life I want?
- Do they inspire me—or make me doubt myself?

Write your honest answers. If the person wouldn't trade places with you or hasn't taken the risks you're about to take, their advice might be **projection—not protection**.

Step 3: Catch the Ego Trap

Which one of these ego triggers did their words play into?

Circle any that apply:

- They made me feel like I had to **prove** myself.
- They **stroked my ego** to distract me from reflection.
- They made me **doubt my readiness** or uniqueness.
- They used **fear** to make me second-guess myself.
- They made me feel **guilty** for growing.

What effect did it have on you?

"After they said that, I started to..."

(e.g., hesitate, shrink my idea, feel unsure, self-sabotage, etc.)

Step 4: Flip the Power Dynamic

Choose ONE limiting statement they gave you and reframe it with truth:

"They said _____, but I know _____."

Example: *"They said this might not work out—but I know I'd rather try and grow than stay stuck wondering."*

Then affirm your independence:

"Their fear is not my future."

"Their limitations don't define me."

"Their doubt isn't my reality."

(Choose one or create your own power mantra.)

Step 5: Commit to Listening to Winners

Write the name of someone who *has* done what you're trying to do—or someone whose mindset inspires you to grow (this could be a mentor, author, speaker, or even your future self):

"From now on, I take advice from _____ because they reflect the kind of success I want."

Reminder:

You don't need to be liked to be great.

You don't need approval to be successful.

And you don't need to stay small to make other people comfortable.

Your growth is your responsibility—not theirs. Your power is yours—*reclaim it.*

Final Thoughts: Reclaiming Your Power from Ego-Based Manipulation

People will always have opinions about your life. Some will **support you wholeheartedly.** Some will **doubt you quietly.** And some will **secretly hope you fail.**

But the most dangerous thing?

Letting someone else's words control your actions.

The moment you start **filtering your decisions through the fears, doubts, and insecurities of others, you hand over your power.** You let their limitations become your reality. You let their small-mindedness shape your future.

It's time to take your power back.

Stop seeking permission.

No one else has to approve of your path. If you know where you're going, that's enough.

Stop letting fear-based advice stop you.

Most people don't operate from a place of vision. They operate from fear, survival, and playing it safe. Don't let their small thinking shrink your dreams.

Stop staying small to make other people comfortable.

Your success will make some people uncomfortable. **That's their problem, not yours.** Playing small doesn't serve you, and it sure as hell doesn't serve the world.

Because at the end of the day, **your success isn't about them. It's about you.**

And the more you step into your power, the less their opinions will matter.

Chapter 16: The Key to Long-Term Success – Balancing Confidence & Humility

Success is a double-edged sword.

On one side, **confidence** is what drives you forward. It helps you take risks, believe in yourself, and push past obstacles that might stop others. It fuels your ambition and gives you the courage to go after what you want.

But on the other side, **ego** can be your downfall. It can make you arrogant, closed-minded, and blind to your own weaknesses. It can trick you into thinking you don't need to improve, that you've already "made it," or that you're above learning from others.

The people who reach real, lasting success aren't just confident—they're also humble.

They understand that:

Being willing to learn is more powerful than pretending to know everything.

The moment you stop learning, you stop growing. The most successful people aren't the ones who *think* they know it all—they're the ones who stay curious, seek knowledge, and constantly evolve.

Feedback is a tool for growth, not an attack.

A fragile ego takes criticism personally. A strong mind uses it as fuel. Learning how to accept constructive feedback without getting defensive is one of the most valuable skills for long-term success.

Success without self-awareness leads to self-destruction. Many talented, intelligent, and powerful people have lost everything—not because they weren't good at what they did, but because they let arrogance, ignorance, or unchecked ego get in the way. Staying grounded and self-aware is what keeps success sustainable.

The Challenge: Balancing Confidence & Humility
True power comes from striking the right balance:
- **Confidence** gives you the courage to take action.
- **Humility** keeps you open to learning and growth.

The key is knowing how to stay **bold and ambitious** without letting ego sabotage you along the way. This chapter will break down how to build unshakable confidence while staying humble enough to keep winning—because real success isn't just about *getting* to the top, it's about *staying* there.

Why Being Willing to Learn is More Powerful Than Pretending to Know Everything
Ego wants to prove.
Confidence wants to improve.
That's the difference.
There's a massive gap between:
Fake confidence – acting like you have all the answers, refusing to be questioned, and pretending to know more than you do.

True confidence – knowing that you *don't* have all the answers but being willing to learn, adapt, and grow.
The most successful people in the world? They **never stop learning.**

Warren Buffett still reads and studies every day, despite being one of the greatest investors of all time. He knows that no matter how much he's accomplished, there's always more to learn.

Kobe Bryant was at the top of his game, but he still studied other players, practiced relentlessly, and absorbed knowledge from anyone who could help him improve.

Elon Musk dives into industries he isn't even trained in, constantly expanding his knowledge and surrounding himself with experts to learn from.

Meanwhile, people with **fragile egos** stop learning the moment they think they've "made it." They get complacent, they reject new ideas, and they prioritize being *right* over getting *better*.

And the result? **The second you believe you have nothing left to learn, you start declining.**

Because real power doesn't come from knowing everything—it comes from being **willing to learn anything.**

How to Stay Open to Feedback Without Letting Ego Take Over

Ego hates feedback. It sees it as an **attack** instead of an **opportunity.**

That's why most people:

Get defensive instead of listening. They hear feedback and immediately feel the need to argue, justify, or explain themselves instead of actually considering it.

Make excuses instead of improving. Instead of owning their mistakes, they blame the circumstances, the other person, or anything but themselves.

Only listen to praise and ignore constructive criticism. Compliments feel good, but growth comes from hearing what you *need* to hear—not just what you *want* to hear.

But the people who go the farthest?

Actively seek feedback from those they respect. They don't just wait for criticism—they go out of their way to ask for it from mentors, experts, and people who can genuinely help them improve.

Use criticism as a tool to get better. Instead of seeing it as an attack, they see it as an opportunity to level up.

Detach their worth from their performance. They understand that making a mistake doesn't make them a failure. They separate who they are from what they do—so feedback doesn't feel like a personal attack.

How to Make Feedback Work for You

1. Pause before reacting.

Your first instinct might be to defend yourself, explain why they're wrong, or shut down completely. Instead, take a breath. Let the feedback sink in before responding.

2. Ask yourself: "Is this coming from someone I respect?"

Not all feedback is worth listening to. If it's coming from someone who has experience, knowledge, or genuine insight, it's worth considering. If not, don't take it personally.

3. **Extract the lesson.**

Even if the feedback isn't delivered perfectly, there's *usually* something valuable in it. Instead of focusing on how it was said, focus on what you can learn from it.

4. **Apply it and move forward.**

The goal isn't just to *hear* feedback—it's to use it. Growth happens when you make adjustments, not when you argue or dismiss criticism.

The faster you learn to take feedback **without ego,** the faster you improve. Because in the end, **it's not about being perfect—it's about always getting better.**

How to Achieve Success Without Ego Destroying You in the Process

Success isn't just about **getting there.** It's about **staying there.**

And if there's one thing that destroys success faster than failure itself, it's **ego.**

Ego makes people complacent. It makes them stop learning, stop evolving, and stop listening. It convinces them they've "arrived," when in reality, **the moment you think you've made it is the moment you start falling.**

So how do you build **lasting** success without self-sabotaging along the way?

How to Stay Successful Without Letting Ego Take Over

Stay a student, no matter how successful you become.

The most powerful people in the world **never stop learning.** No matter how much you accomplish, there's always something new to master. Growth is a lifelong process.

Surround yourself with people who challenge you.

Avoid "yes-men" and fake supporters who only tell you what you *want* to hear. True allies push you to be better, call you out when necessary, and hold you to a higher standard.

Detach from external validation.

If you need **constant** praise and approval, ego is still running the show. Real confidence comes from within—not from people clapping for you.

Prioritize growth over proving yourself.

Winning means nothing if you're not improving. **Focus on progress, not perfection.** The best competitors don't just aim to be the best today—they work to be even better tomorrow.

The Ultimate Balance: Confidence + Humility

Confidence = *I trust myself.*

Humility = *I know I still have more to learn.*

When you **combine** the two, you become:

Unstoppable – because you believe in yourself.

Respected – because you stay grounded and open to growth.

Always evolving – because you never stop improving.

That's the **real** secret to long-term success.

Stay hungry. Stay humble. Stay winning.

Exercise: The Confidence + Humility Alignment Check

To help you assess where you're operating from genuine confidence and where ego might be quietly getting in the way—and build a healthier foundation for long-term success.

Step 1: Rate Yourself Honestly

For each statement, rate yourself from **1 (rarely true)** to **5 (always true)**:

I believe in myself even when others doubt me.

I stay open to feedback, even when it's uncomfortable.

I seek out people who challenge me to be better.

I can admit when I don't know something without feeling insecure.

I take criticism as an opportunity, not an insult.

I trust my abilities without needing to prove myself to everyone.

I celebrate wins—but stay focused on continued growth.

Total Score: _____ / 35

- **30–35:** You're flowing in aligned confidence and humility—keep going!

- **20–29:** You're doing great but may need to check in with your ego more often.
- **Below 20:** Time to refocus on growth over proving. This chapter is your blueprint.

Step 2: Spot the Imbalance

Ask yourself:

Where am I leaning too far into ego right now?

(e.g., "I've been brushing off feedback at work because I feel like I should already know everything.")

Where could I be more confident in myself, without needing external validation?

(e.g., "I keep asking for reassurance when I already know I'm doing the right thing.")

Step 3: Balance It Out

Now, write one intention for each trait:

- **Confidence:**
  "This week, I will back myself by..." (e.g., *Trusting my ideas in meetings without second-guessing them.*)
- **Humility:**
  "This week, I will stay open by..." (e.g., *Asking for feedback from someone I respect and actually listening.*)

Step 4: Lock It In With a Grounding Mantra

Pick one or create your own:

- "I am confident in who I am and humble enough to keep growing."
- "My strength is in knowing there's always more to learn."
- "I don't have to be perfect to be powerful."

Say it. Feel it. Let it guide your next step.

Reminder:

Mastery isn't about being the best—it's about being your best, every day.

Let confidence push you forward.

Let humility keep you growing.

That's how you stay on top without falling off.

Final Thoughts: The Most Powerful People Master Ego—Not the Other Way Around

At the end of the day, success isn't just about **skills, hard work, or even confidence.**

It's about mastering your own **ego.**

Because the moment you stop chasing status, proving yourself, and seeking validation—something shifts.

You free up energy to actually become great.

Instead of wasting energy worrying about how you're perceived, you focus on *becoming* the person who deserves success.

You stop letting the fear of failure hold you back.

Ego makes failure feel personal. But once you let go of ego, failure becomes what it truly is—a lesson, a stepping stone, just another part of the process.

You step into your power fully—without arrogance, but with certainty.

Confidence without ego is the ultimate advantage. You don't have to prove anything—you *are* something. And that's what makes people take notice.

This is what separates the ones who **truly** make it from the ones who **peak too soon.**

Because **real success?** It's not just about **how high you climb—** it's about **how well you sustain it.**

Chapter 17: The Ego in Apologies – Saying Sorry Without Losing Yourself

Let's talk about the word so many people choke on: **"Sorry."**

Ego hates it.

Ego sees it as surrender.

As weakness.

As an admission of failure.

But here's the truth:

Saying "I'm sorry" isn't weak — it's one of the strongest things you can do.

The ego will try to convince you that apologizing means you're "giving away power." That you're letting someone "win." That it'll make you look small or submissive.

But that's a lie.

The *real* loss of power happens when you refuse to take accountability and let your ego sabotage trust, respect, and connection.

Because people don't remember if you messed up — they remember if you refused to own it.

Why Ego Fears Apologies

The ego is obsessed with being right.

It's not interested in growth — it's interested in control.

It doesn't want peace — it wants to win.

To the ego, an apology feels like a loss. Like giving up power. Like admitting you're flawed, and that scares the hell out of it. So instead of choosing honesty, it chooses deflection.

Instead of saying, *"I hurt you and I take responsibility,"* ego will dress it up and deflect it like this:

- *"I'm sorry you feel that way."*
- *"I didn't mean it, so you shouldn't be mad."*
- *"I guess I'll apologize, but I don't think I did anything wrong."*
- *"I'm sorry, but..."*

Each of these is a half-apology — a weak handshake covered in pride.

It sounds like accountability, but it's just ego trying to protect itself from the discomfort of being seen as "wrong."

But here's the truth: **you can be wrong and still be lovable.**

You can mess up and still be a good person.

You can take ownership of your actions *without sacrificing your self-respect.*

The ego acts like being wrong means being unworthy — like your entire value crumbles the moment you admit fault. But real strength is built on humility, not perfection.

Saying "I'm sorry" doesn't mean you're giving up power — it means you're *taking ownership* of the power you actually have:

The power to repair.

The power to grow.

The power to lead with integrity instead of image.

The ego can't stand discomfort — but growth *lives there.*

And when you learn how to apologize without defending your pride? That's when you know ego's no longer in the driver's seat.

Genuine Apology vs. Ego-Driven Manipulation

Let's get one thing straight: **a real apology isn't about being right — it's about making it right.**

It's not about cleaning up your *image* — it's about cleaning up your *impact*.

A genuine apology is centered on the *other person's experience.* It's grounded in empathy, responsibility, and a willingness to repair.

An ego-driven apology, on the other hand, isn't an apology at all — it's a performance. A PR move. A way to quiet the noise without actually hearing what someone's trying to say. It's more about *relieving your own discomfort* than honoring someone else's pain.

Let's break it down:

Genuine Apology:

- *"I'm sorry I hurt you. That wasn't my intention, but I take full responsibility."*
  You acknowledge harm was done, even if it wasn't on purpose.
- *"I can see how my actions affected you. Thank you for helping me understand."*
  You're open to seeing from their perspective — not just defending your own.
- *"I care about how you feel, and I want to make it right."*

It's not just words — there's a desire to repair, not just move   on.

This kind of apology builds trust. It shows maturity. It says, *"I value this relationship more than I value my pride."*

Ego-Driven Apology:

- *"I said sorry — what more do you want?"*
  Translation: I'm only here to check a box, not actually make amends.
- *"I'm only apologizing because you're upset."*
  That's not empathy — that's irritation. It shifts the blame instead of taking it.
- *"This wouldn't be a problem if you weren't so sensitive."*
  This invalidates the other person's experience and centers your ego's need to feel "reasonable."

These types of apologies are dismissive, defensive, and manipulative.
They sound like accountability on the surface — but underneath, it's all ego trying to maintain control.

See the difference?

One opens a door — it invites connection, healing, and growth.
The other slams it shut, locks it, and pretends it was never there in the first place.
A real apology takes *courage.*

It means facing the discomfort of being seen, being called in, being wrong.

But it's in that moment — *that* exact place where your pride wants to run — that real respect is built.

Because the goal of an apology is not to escape the discomfort. The goal is to move *through* it — and come out the other side with more clarity, connection, and integrity than before.

How Accountability Builds Real Strength and Respect

We live in a world where deflection is the norm. Where people double down on their mistakes instead of owning them. Where silence, ghosting, or defensiveness is easier than facing discomfort. But when you choose to rise above that?

When you own your actions — something powerful happens.

- **You grow.**
  You become more self-aware. You evolve. You learn how to respond instead of react, and how to hold space for both your own truth *and* someone else's experience.

- **You earn trust.**
  People feel safer around you. They know you're not just going to defend your pride — you're going to show up with integrity, even when it's uncomfortable.

- **You create emotional safety.**
  You send the message: *"You can be honest with me, and I won't punish you for it."* That's rare. That's real. That's how connection deepens.

- **You become reliable — not just when things are good, but when they're messy.**

  Anyone can show up when it's easy. But the people who stay accountable during conflict? That's leadership. That's maturity. That's strength.

Because here's the truth:

Accountability doesn't make you small. It makes you *solid*.

It proves that your character isn't built on perfection — it's built on *honesty*, *growth*, and the ability to take responsibility without crumbling under it.

It takes *zero courage* to defend yourself.

To deflect, justify, or shift blame.

That's the ego's default.

But it takes *emotional maturity* to say:

- *"I was wrong, and I'm still worthy."*
- *"I hurt you, and I care enough to repair it."*
- *"I can apologize without losing myself."*

That's power.

That's growth.

That's ego in check — and self-respect turned all the way up.

The Apology Archetypes – How Ego Shows Up in Disguise

Not all ego is loud and obvious. Sometimes, it hides behind "good intentions," passive behaviors, or polished language. These common apology archetypes help you recognize when ego is still driving the apology—even if it sounds "nice."

The Defender

"I'm sorry, but I was just trying to help."

This one loves to sneak in a justification. The apology is always followed by a defense. It sounds like ownership, but it's really just image protection.

Reframe: "I see now that my impact hurt you—even if I meant well."

The Peacemaker

"Okay okay, I'm sorry. Can we just move on?"

This one isn't apologizing for growth—they're apologizing for peace. They hate tension more than they value understanding. It's a rush to resolution without real accountability.

Reframe: "I want to understand where I went wrong. Your feelings matter to me."

The Performer

"I'm so sorry, I feel terrible, I'm the worst person ever..."

This one makes the apology about themselves. It turns the conversation into a pity party so they don't have to sit with the discomfort of someone else's pain.

Reframe: "I hurt you, and I care about making it right—what do you need from me?"

The Ghost

They disappear instead of apologizing at all. Then they pop up like nothing happened. This isn't avoidance—it's ego shielding itself from accountability.

Reframe: "I disappeared when I should've shown up. I take responsibility for that."

The Genuinely Accountable

This one takes full ownership. No excuses. No pity. Just presence, growth, and emotional maturity.

Mantra: "I was wrong, I care, and I'm willing to repair."

Which one have *you* been? (We've all been at least one. The goal isn't perfection—it's awareness.)

What Ego Says vs. What Accountability Sounds Like

Here's a side-by-side to help you check yourself in the moment.

Ego Says:

"I said sorry, what more do you want?"

"I didn't mean to, so it shouldn't matter."

"I guess I'll say sorry if that's what you need."

"You're taking this too personally."

"Fine, I'm sorry."

Accountability Says:

"I want to repair the damage I caused, not just move past it."

"I didn't mean to—but I see how it still hurt you."

"I care about your feelings. I want to make this right."

"Even if I wouldn't have reacted the same, your feelings are valid."

"I take full accountability. I understand why you feel the way you do."

The shift is subtle—but everything changes when your focus moves from *defending yourself* to *understanding them*.

The 3-Step Grounded Apology Formula

This is your go-to for apologizing like the version of you who leads with growth, not ego.

1. Acknowledge the Impact

"I understand that what I did hurt you—even if that wasn't my intention."

This shows empathy. It proves you're focused on their experience, not just your own defense.

2. Own the Responsibility

"That was my choice. I take full accountability."

Don't sugarcoat it. No justifications. No "but." Just honesty. That's what builds trust.

3. Offer Repair

"I care about our connection, and I want to make this right. Is there anything I can do to rebuild trust?"

This keeps the conversation open and empowers the other person to share what they need from you.

You don't have to script every word—but if your apology includes all three of these, it's coming from a place of strength, not ego.

How to Receive an Apology Without Feeding Someone's Ego

Real apologies are about repair—not redemption. So if someone apologizes to you, here's how to respond without abandoning your boundaries.

- **You can accept an apology without rushing forgiveness.**
  It's okay to say: *"Thank you for the apology. I need time to process it."*

- **You can acknowledge the gesture without dismissing the harm.**
  Say: *"I appreciate your apology—and I'm still hurt. We'll need time to rebuild."*

- **You're allowed to require changed behavior, not just words.**
  Apology without growth is just a performance. Real healing takes consistency.

This protects your peace *and* keeps the ego out of both sides of the equation.

Final Affirmations – Apologizing Without Losing Yourself

Repeat these. Let them sit in your chest. Say them out loud if you need to.

- "I can be wrong and still be worthy."
- "Accountability doesn't weaken me—it strengthens my integrity."
- "I lead with honesty, not ego."
- "I don't have to be perfect to be powerful."
- "My apology isn't about image—it's about impact."

Reflective Exercise: Apology Check-In – Ego or Accountability?

This exercise is all about self-awareness — not shame. The goal isn't to judge yourself, but to *observe yourself* and grow. Think of a time you apologized (or didn't) and reflect honestly:

1. **Did I take full responsibility, or was I trying to defend myself while apologizing?**
   (Be honest. Did you say "but"? Did you try to make them understand your side more than hear theirs?)
2. **What was I really afraid of when I avoided or watered down the apology?**
   (Being wrong? Being rejected? Looking weak?)
3. **Did my apology center their experience, or was I trying to manage how I looked?**
4. **If I were to apologize again, from a grounded and ego-free place, what would I say differently?**

5. What kind of person do I want to be in conflict — defensive and image-focused, or honest and growth-oriented?

Bonus Prompt:
"What does a strong, grounded apology sound like from the version of me who isn't trying to be perfect — just real?"

Write it. Sit with it. Practice being that version of you.

Final Words: The Apology Isn't the Weakness — the Ego Is

Apologizing doesn't make you smaller.

It makes you *braver.*

It means you're strong enough to face the mirror and *still love who you see.*

You don't have to be perfect to be powerful.

You don't have to be "right" to be respected.

And you don't lose yourself when you say "I'm sorry" — you *find* the version of you that's actually worth becoming.

Let your ego shrink so your character can rise.

Because real power isn't in always being right — it's in being real.

Part 5: The Real-Life Battle

How We All Struggle with Ego (and How to Overcome It)

This isn't just a concept—it's real life. Ego shows up in the everyday moments: when you're triggered, when you want to be right, when you feel rejected, when your pride gets bruised. It's not just some abstract idea—it's personal, messy, and sometimes hard to spot in the moment.

We all struggle with ego. Every single one of us. The goal isn't to get rid of it completely—that's not realistic. The goal is to recognize it when it's running the show and learn how to choose differently.

This part of the book is about *you*—your patterns, your challenges, your growth. It's about catching ego in action and learning how to respond from a place of awareness, not automatic reaction. We're not aiming for perfection here. We're aiming for presence. Progress. Peace.

Because the truth is: ego may be loud, but it's not who you are. And the more you start seeing it clearly, the less power it has over your life.

Let's get real about the battle—and how to rise above it.

Chapter 18: When Ego Ruins Relationships

Ego isn't just a personal struggle—it's a **relationship killer.**

It turns **small misunderstandings into full-blown fights.** It makes people **choose being right over being happy.** It fuels **defensiveness, pride, and emotional triggers**—all of which destroy real connection.

If you've ever:

Felt the need to **have the last word.**

Held onto **grudges** instead of resolving issues.

Gotten **defensive** instead of actually listening.

Then you've seen **ego in action.**

The problem? **Most people don't even realize when ego is running the show.** They think they're just "standing their ground" or "protecting themselves," but in reality, they're pushing people away.

The good news? **The moment you recognize how ego affects relationships, you can start communicating in a way that actually deepens trust, understanding, and connection.**

This chapter is about breaking down the most common ways ego shows up in relationships—and more importantly, how to **get out of your own way** to create stronger, healthier connections.

How Ego Causes Unnecessary Conflicts

Not every disagreement needs to turn into a battle—but **ego loves turning conversations into competitions.**

Someone disagrees with you? Ego sees it as an *attack* instead of a difference in perspective.

Someone calls you out? Ego makes you *defend* instead of *reflect*.

Someone expresses their feelings? Ego makes it *about you* instead of actually *listening*.

And that's how small misunderstandings turn into full-blown fights.

Most arguments **aren't really about the issue at hand.** They're about:

Feeling unheard, unappreciated, or disrespected.

People don't just want to be right—they want to be *understood*. But when ego takes over, listening stops, and defensiveness takes its place.

Needing to "win" the argument instead of solving the problem.

Ego isn't focused on resolution—it's focused on *domination*. When the goal is to *win* instead of *understand*, both people lose.

Reacting emotionally instead of seeking clarity.

Instead of asking, *What did they really mean?* or *How can we fix this?*, ego makes you jump to conclusions, assume the worst, and react impulsively.

But when you **let go of ego-driven reactions,** everything changes.

You start communicating in a way that actually **builds relationships—not damages them.**

You start listening to **understand—not just to respond.** And most importantly, you start realizing that **the goal isn't to be right—it's to be connected.**

How to Handle Ego-Driven Fights and Emotional Triggers

Ego thrives in **heated moments.** It pushes you to react instantly, defend yourself aggressively, and fight to "win" instead of actually resolving anything. But when you learn to **catch it in the moment,** you regain control—not just over the argument, but over yourself.

Here's how to **break the cycle** and shift from **ego-driven reactions to real connection.**

1. Pause Before Reacting

Ego makes you **fire back immediately** when you feel criticized or challenged. It fuels emotional, impulsive reactions that often make things worse.

Winning move:

Instead of reacting emotionally, **take a breath.** Ask yourself: **"Am I responding with understanding or with ego?"** Delay your response if you feel triggered—give yourself **time to process** before speaking.

Why it works:

When you pause, you stop letting ego **control the conversation.** You give yourself the space to **respond with intention** instead of reacting with emotion.

2. Stop Taking Everything Personally

Not everything is an attack. **Sometimes, it's just someone expressing their perspective.** But ego makes you assume **every disagreement is about you**—even when it's not.

Winning move:

Instead of thinking, **"They're attacking me,"** shift to **"They're sharing how they feel."**

Remember that **their emotions aren't about your worth.** You don't have to internalize everything.

Let go of the need to **defend every little thing.** Not every statement requires a response.

Why it works:

When you stop taking things personally, you create space for **real understanding** instead of unnecessary tension. Most people just want to be *heard*—not to hurt you.

3. Focus on Understanding, Not Winning

Most fights **escalate** because both people are trying to be **right.** But relationships aren't competitions—**and winning the argument often means losing the connection.**

Winning move:

Instead of proving your point, ask: **"What's the deeper issue here?"**

Instead of thinking, **"How can I win?"** ask **"How can we both feel heard?"**

Let go of your **need for control**—and choose connection instead.

Why it works:

The strongest relationships **aren't built on power struggles.** They're built on **mutual understanding, respect, and the ability to communicate without ego leading the way.**

The Bottom Line

Ego wants control. But real strength comes from choosing connection over control.

The next time you feel triggered, **pause, reflect, and respond with self-awareness.** That's how you turn conflicts into **opportunities for deeper connection**—instead of battles where nobody truly wins.

How to Communicate with Understanding Instead of Defensiveness

One of the biggest relationship killers? **Listening just to respond instead of listening to understand.**

Ego makes conversations feel like battles—it urges you to **defend, justify, and prove your point.** But real connection comes from **mutual understanding, not from "winning."**

Here's how to shift from **ego-driven defensiveness** to **communication that actually strengthens relationships.**

1. Listen First, Respond Later

Most people listen **just to reply**—waiting for their turn to talk instead of actually processing what the other person is saying.

Winning move:

Focus on *hearing* what they're saying—not on formulating your response.

Pause before speaking. Let their words fully register before jumping in.

Validate their emotions before introducing your perspective.

Why it works:

When people feel heard, they're more open to hearing *you* in return.

2. Acknowledge Their Feelings Before Making Your Point

If someone expresses frustration, hurt, or disappointment, ego **immediately** wants to explain why they're wrong. But when you skip over their emotions, they feel dismissed.

Winning move:

Instead of jumping to *your* side, start with *theirs.*

Say: **"I hear you. I understand why you feel that way."** Let them know you've processed their words before offering your response.

Why it works:

People don't just want solutions—they want **validation** that their emotions are real and respected.

3. Drop the "But"

Ever notice how **"I understand, but..."** instantly makes the other person defensive? That's because *everything before the "but"* gets erased the moment you say it.

Winning move:

Replace "but" with **"and."** Example:

Instead of: *"I understand, but I didn't mean it that way."*

Say: **"I understand, and I'd like to share my perspective too."**

Why it works:

"And" keeps both perspectives valid. "But" dismisses theirs in favor of yours.

4. Ask Clarifying Questions Instead of Assuming

Ego loves to assume. It makes you react before you even know what the other person actually needs.

Winning move:

Instead of guessing, ask: **"What do you need from me right now?"**

If something isn't clear, say: **"Can you help me understand this better?"**

Approach the conversation with curiosity, not judgment.

Why it works:

Assumptions create **misunderstandings.** Asking questions creates **clarity.**

Signs You're Mastering Ego in Relationships

You resolve conflicts faster.

You no longer let minor disagreements drag on because you're not fueling them with ego.

You don't feel the need to "win" arguments.

You prioritize understanding over proving a point.

You listen with an open heart instead of reacting defensively.

You hear people out without feeling personally attacked.

You choose connection over control.

Instead of forcing your way, you focus on finding **common ground.**

The Bottom Line

When you **communicate to understand instead of to defend,** relationships strengthen.

Drop the ego, stay open, and remember: **It's not you vs. them— it's both of you vs. the problem.**

The Ego Roles in Relationships

Sometimes, ego doesn't scream—it *hides* behind roles that feel justified.

It convinces you that you're being helpful, protective, or rational, when really, it's just scared of being vulnerable, wrong, or out of control.

Here are three common ego roles you might be slipping into without realizing it:

1. The Fixer

This role looks helpful on the surface—but it's ego trying to stay in control.

How it shows up:

You always try to "solve" their emotions instead of listening. You jump into solution mode so fast that they never feel heard. You don't mean to dismiss them—but that's how it feels.

Example:

"They're upset, so I'll tell them how to fix it."

Translation: *"I don't know how to sit in discomfort, so I'll take control of the conversation instead."*

The upgrade:

Become the Listener.

You don't have to fix everything. Sometimes, the most healing thing you can do is say, "That sounds really hard. I'm here."

2. The Controller

This one is driven by fear. Fear of uncertainty. Fear of losing power. Fear of not being heard.

So you dominate the conversation, steer the direction, and try to make sure it all goes your way.

How it shows up:

You interrupt. You redirect. You talk more than you listen. You might even be "right"—but no one feels safe or connected with you.

Example:

"If I don't stay in control, I might get hurt."

Translation: *"I'd rather win the conversation than feel the vulnerability of not knowing how it'll go."*

The upgrade:

Become the Collaborator.

Let the other person lead sometimes. Share the mic. Ask, "What do *you* need from this conversation?"

3. The Avoider

Instead of ego making you loud—it makes you silent. You shut down, disappear, or brush it off when things get uncomfortable.

How it shows up:

You ghost mid-convo. You say "I'm fine" when you're not. You'd rather retreat than risk confrontation, but unresolved emotions keep building beneath the surface.

Example:
"It's better to say nothing than make things worse." Translation: *"I'm afraid of the discomfort that comes with honest connection."*

The upgrade:
Become the Resolver.

Conflict isn't a threat—it's a doorway to understanding. Say, "I don't know how to fix this yet, but I want to talk about it."

We've all played these roles at some point.
The goal isn't perfection—it's awareness.
And once you see the role you've been playing, you can choose to play a better one.

Conflict With Ego vs. Conflict With Clarity

Here's a simple breakdown to help you recognize what kind of energy you're bringing into a disagreement.

Conflict With Ego
Interrupts and reacts
Assumes intention
Says "You always/never…"
Brings up old baggage
Needs to "win"
Defends pride

Protects connection
Avoids discomfort

Conflict With Clarity
Listens and pauses
Asks for clarification
Says "I feel ___ when ___"
Stays focused on the issue
Wants to understand
Embraces growth conversations

The shift is simple, but powerful.
Ego argues.
Clarity connects.

Affirmation Block: The Relationship Reset
Start your day or end a tough conversation with these. Let them ground you before your next response.

- "I choose understanding over ego."
- "I don't need to be right—I want to be connected."
- "I release the need to control the conversation."
- "It's safe to pause, listen, and respond with care."
- "My relationships grow when I do."
- "I can communicate without defending my pride."
- "Love isn't about winning—it's about understanding."
- "I let go of power plays and choose mutual peace."

Exercise: Ego or Intimacy? A Relationship Conflict Decoder

To help you recognize when ego is taking over during a disagreement—and practice responding with connection, not control.

Step 1: Reflect on a Recent Conflict

. Think of a recent disagreement you had with someone (romantic, family, friend, or work-related). Briefly describe what happened:

"The conflict was about..."

"What I wanted in that moment was..."

Step 2: Spot the Ego Moves

Check off anything you did during or after the disagreement:

Reacted instantly without pausing

Tried to prove your point instead of listening

Got defensive when they shared how they felt

Avoided the conversation instead of resolving it

Focused more on being right than being understood

Took their words personally

Used "but" when validating their feelings

Brought up past mistakes to defend yourself

Now ask:

"What was my ego protecting in that moment?"

(e.g., my pride, my need to be respected, my image, my fear of being wrong)

Step 3: Reframe It With Emotional Maturity

Rewrite your response—this time with connection, not ego.

"Instead of reacting, I could have said..." (e.g., "I hear you. That wasn't my intention, and I want to understand where you're coming from.")

"If I had led with understanding instead of defense, the outcome might have been..."

Step 4: Create a Go-To Connection Mantra

Pick one or write your own:

- "I don't need to win—I want to understand."
- "I respond to connect, not to control."
- "My ego doesn't speak for my heart."
- "Pause. Breathe. Then choose clarity."

Optional: Relationship Reset Challenge

Challenge yourself for the next 3 conversations—especially ones that could get tense—to:

1. **Pause before responding.**
2. **Validate the other person's feelings first.**
3. **Replace "but" with "and."**
4. **Ask one clarifying question.**

Journal how each conversation felt different and what you learned about yourself.

Final Thoughts: Ego Doesn't Build Relationships—It Destroys Them

At the end of the day, **ego will always try to make you react, defend, and control.** It will push you to prove a point instead of **understanding** one. It will make you hold onto grudges instead of **resolving** them. It will convince you that being right is more important than being **connected.**

But the **strongest relationships?** They aren't built on pride, competition, or stubbornness.

They are built on:

Communication, patience, and self-awareness.

Healthy relationships require effort—not to "win" but to **understand.** When both people commit to listening, reflecting, and adjusting, conflicts turn into growth opportunities.

Thriving when both people listen instead of argue.

The best relationships aren't the ones with **zero disagreements**—they're the ones where disagreements are handled with **respect, clarity, and emotional intelligence.**

Growing when you let go of pride and choose understanding.

When you replace **ego-driven reactions** with **conscious responses,** you create space for **deeper connection and mutual respect.**

Because the people who **master ego in relationships** don't just **avoid unnecessary fights**—they build relationships that are **stronger, healthier, and more fulfilling.**

241

That's the difference between love that lasts and love that burns out.

Chapter 19: Breaking Free from Ego's Control in Everyday Life

Ego isn't just something that shows up in big moments—it influences **every single day** of your life.

It makes you:

Rewrite history—twisting events to protect your pride.

Misinterpret reality—making things seem worse (or better) than they really were.

Reject real support—because it doesn't always come in the form your ego wants.

The danger? **If you don't recognize these patterns, ego will keep you stuck in false narratives, toxic cycles, and missed opportunities for growth.**

But once you learn how to separate **truth from ego's distortions,** you gain full control over your thoughts, emotions, and future.

How Ego Makes You Rewrite History
Twisting Events in Your Mind

Ego isn't interested in facts—it's interested in protecting your self-image.

Its main goal is simple: *preserve your pride.* And to do that, it will rewrite entire moments in your mind, framing you in the most flattering light—even if it means distorting reality.

That's why the ego:

Casts you as the victim in every situation where you were challenged.

Elevates you to the hero in stories where you may have hurt others. Labels you the misunderstood genius anytime someone didn't agree with you.

It edits the past like a biased movie director—cutting out scenes that show your flaws, exaggerating moments that feed your pride, and blurring anything that would force you to take real accountability.

But here's the truth:

- You weren't always right.
- You weren't always wronged.
- And you weren't always as innocent—or as guilty—as you remember.

Ego rewrites history to protect itself.
Growth, though? Growth requires honesty.
Not just honesty with others—but the kind that starts with *you*.

How to Stop Twisting the Past

You can't change what happened—but you *can* change how you see it.

Here's how to start breaking free from ego's mental edits:
Ask yourself:

"Am I remembering this accurately... or in a way that protects my pride?"

This one question can open the door to a whole new level of self-awareness.

Flip the perspective:

"If they told this story, how would it sound?"

Not to invalidate your feelings—but to expand your understanding.

Separate facts from feelings:

Memory is deeply emotional. But emotions aren't evidence.

Ask: *"What actually happened? What did I feel? What might they have felt?"*

Notice the patterns:

Do you always come out of your memories as the one who was "right"?

That's a sign your ego might be doing the editing.

Practice grace and accountability at the same time.

It's not about beating yourself up—it's about being real with yourself, so you can actually grow.

When you stop letting ego filter the past, you start learning the real lessons from your experiences.

You stop defending your image, and start becoming someone you're proud to be—*not just someone you want to appear as.*

That's when healing begins.

That's when clarity comes in.

And that's when you take your power back—not by rewriting the story, but by owning it.

The Difference Between What *Actually* Happened vs. What Ego Wants You to Believe

Ego doesn't want the truth.

It wants *validation*.

It thrives on confirmation bias—meaning it only sees and accepts what supports your existing beliefs. Not because it's trying to lie to you maliciously, but because it's trying to protect your identity, even if that identity is based on pain, pride, or fear.

That's why ego makes everything feel personal—even when it's not.

If you *believe* someone doesn't like you, you'll interpret every neutral action as rejection.

If you *believe* you're always right, you'll ignore moments when you weren't.

If you *believe* you always get screwed over, you'll miss the blessings that did go your way.

If you *believe* people are out to get you, you'll twist even the kindest feedback into an attack.

Ego filters reality to match its story.

But just because something feels true... doesn't mean it *is*.

How to See Reality More Clearly

Seeing clearly doesn't mean dismissing your emotions—it means holding them with honesty instead of ego.

Ask yourself:

"What are the facts, without my emotions attached?"
Try describing the situation like a reporter—just the what, when, where. No assumptions.

Challenge your initial reaction:

"Am I seeing this through truth... or through my ego's story?"
Don't judge the answer. Just notice.

Seek perspective:

Ask a trusted, neutral person: *"How would you see this if it happened to you?"*
Not to give your power away—but to widen your lens.

Practice emotional honesty:

Admit: *"I felt hurt, embarrassed, or rejected"*—but also ask: *"Is that because of what they did, or because of how I interpreted it?"*

The more honest you are about what *actually* happened, the more control you gain over what happens next.

Ego reacts.

Wisdom reflects.

And your peace?

It lives in the space between what you assumed—and what's actually real.

How to Recognize and Appreciate Real, Genuine Support

Ego wants to feel good.

Growth wants to *be* good.

And that's where the tension lies—because real support doesn't always come wrapped in compliments or comfort. Sometimes, it shows up as challenge. As accountability. As a mirror you didn't ask for but absolutely needed.

Ego often resists these moments. It:

Rejects real advice when it doesn't flatter your pride.

Craves praise over productive feedback.

Gets defensive when someone dares to push you higher.

But here's the truth: not all support feels good in the moment—but that doesn't mean it's not love.

Sometimes real support is:

The friend who's willing to be honest with you, even if it's uncomfortable.

The mentor who doesn't coddle you but *believes in your potential* enough to challenge you.

The person who calls you out—not to shame you, but to *wake you up*.

How to Recognize Genuine Support

Not everyone who agrees with you is on your side. And not everyone who challenges you is against you. Here's how to tell if it's real:

Are they invested in my growth—or just my comfort? Real ones want to see you win, even if that means risking the temporary discomfort of tough love.

Does their feedback stretch me—or just soothe me? If someone challenges your patterns with compassion and truth, don't push them away—lean in.

Are they offering perspective—or just validation? Validation can feel nice, but perspective is what leads to evolution.

The more you mature, the more you realize that real support isn't always hype.

Sometimes it's quiet accountability.

Sometimes it's direct truth.

Sometimes it's someone standing beside you saying, *"I know you can do better—so I won't let you settle for less."*

Learn to appreciate those people.

They're not feeding your ego—they're feeding your *elevation*.

Exercise: Ego or Elevation?

Reflecting on the Support Around You

This exercise is about getting honest with yourself—where you've resisted real support, and where you've confused ego-feeding with true growth.

Step 1: Recall a Time You Felt Challenged by Someone's Feedback

- What did they say?
- How did it make you feel in the moment?

- How did you respond—did you get defensive, dismiss them, or take time to reflect?

Step 2: Now, Flip the Script
- Looking back, was their feedback helpful in any way?
- Were they coming from a place of love, honesty, or concern?
- If your ego hadn't reacted, what might you have learned sooner?

Step 3: Audit Your Circle
Use the space below to answer honestly:
- Who in your life tells you the truth, even when it's hard to hear?
- Who hypes you up but never challenges you to grow?
- Who have you pushed away for "not being supportive," when really... they just weren't feeding your ego?

Step 4: Reframe It
Choose one person who offered real support that your ego may have rejected. Write a short message (even if you don't send it) that says:

"Thank you for being honest with me when I didn't want to hear it. I see it differently now, and I appreciate your support more than I realized."

Bonus Reflection:

What kind of support do I want to attract—and how can I become that kind of support for others, too?

Final Thoughts: Mastering Ego = Mastering Life

Ego will always try to:

Rewrite your past.

Filter your reality.

Reject the support that could actually help you.

But the moment you **take control of your ego instead of letting it control you,** you gain:

Clarity. Seeing things as they really are, not how ego wants them to be.

Growth. Learning from the past instead of twisting it to protect your pride.

Stronger relationships. Accepting real support instead of chasing empty validation.

This is the ultimate key to inner peace, self-mastery, and success.

Chapter 20: The Freedom of Mastering Ego

There's a level of peace, confidence, and power that comes **when ego no longer runs your life.**

When you stop:

Reacting emotionally to everything.

Taking things personally.

Feeling like you have to prove yourself.

Life gets easier.

You stop fighting unnecessary battles. You stop wasting energy on things that don't serve you. You start focusing on **what actually matters—your growth, happiness, and purpose.**

The moment you master ego, **you unlock a level of freedom most people never experience.**

How Overcoming Ego Makes Life Easier, More Peaceful, and Fulfilling

Ego complicates everything.

It turns small issues into heavy burdens.

It makes conversations feel like battles.

It makes you overthink, overreact, and overextend—just to protect a version of yourself that isn't even real.

When ego is in control, life feels like a constant performance. You're always trying to prove something. Win something. Defend something.

But once you start loosening ego's grip... *everything* shifts.

You realize:

You don't have to take things so personally. Not everything is an attack. Not everything needs a reaction. People are living their own stories—and most of the time, their actions have nothing to do with you.

You don't have to react to every challenge or opinion. Silence becomes power. Stillness becomes strength. You stop wasting energy on proving your worth—and start living like you already have it.

You don't have to carry the emotional weight of old wounds, grudges, or pride.

You start letting go—not out of weakness, but because peace matters more than being "right."

The Result?
Less stress.

You're not drained by drama or triggered by every little thing.

More emotional control.

You respond with clarity instead of reacting out of defensiveness.

Deeper connections.

You stop keeping people at arm's length to protect your image—and start allowing real intimacy, honesty, and mutual growth.

A quiet kind of confidence.

You don't need validation to feel enough. You *are* enough.

A sense of peace no one can take from you.

Because it's not dependent on your ego—it's rooted in your truth.

When ego stops running the show, life stops feeling like a fight.

You move with intention.

You listen with openness.

You love without conditions.

And most importantly... you finally feel *free*.

That's what it means to live without ego as your master. That's what it means to come home to yourself.

The Joy of Growth

When You Realize You're Not the Same Person You Used to Be

One day, without even trying to make it happen, you'll look back and realize how much you've changed. And not in a loud, dramatic way—but in a quiet, soul-deep kind of way.

The things that used to trigger you?

They don't bother you anymore. You've outgrown the need to react.

The validation you used to chase?

It doesn't hold power over you. You're rooted in your own worth now.

The conflicts you used to engage in?

They feel heavy, unnecessary—even beneath you. Peace became more valuable than proving a point.

And that's when you know:

You've grown.

Not just mentally—but emotionally, spiritually, energetically.

The best part?

You won't feel the need to announce it.

There's no need to post about it, prove it, or make anyone notice.

Because real growth doesn't scream.

It just *moves differently.*

It's in your presence.

Your peace.

Your energy.

Your choices.

You'll know.

And the people meant for your next chapter will feel it too.

How Learning to Manage Ego Leads to True Happiness and Success

When ego runs your life, you're always chasing.

Chasing validation.

Chasing recognition.

Chasing success that checks the boxes—but doesn't actually *fulfill* you.

You're driven by what things look like, not how they *feel.*

You measure success by applause instead of alignment.

You confuse confidence with performance.

And happiness? It always feels just out of reach—because ego keeps moving the finish line.

But once you learn to manage ego—not silence it, but *master* it—you start to see things differently.

True success isn't about appearances. It's about alignment. It's waking up excited, grounded, and proud of how you live—even if no one's watching.

True confidence isn't about proving anything. It's trusting yourself, even when others don't get it.

True happiness isn't built on attention or approval—it's built on peace, purpose, and presence.

And here's the kicker:

The moment you stop chasing...

You start truly *living*.

Exercise: Ego vs. Alignment

Redefining Success & Happiness on *Your* Terms

This exercise is designed to help you separate what your ego wants... from what your soul truly needs. Because sometimes we chase things without ever asking ourselves *why*.

Step 1: What Are You Chasing Right Now?

List 3 goals, desires, or things you're actively pursuing.

Now for each one, answer:

- *Why do I want this?*
- *Is this for validation, image, or external approval?*
- *Or is this something that feels deeply aligned with who I am and what I value?*

Step 2: What Does *True* Success Look Like to You?

Forget what it's supposed to look like. Forget the pressure. Ask yourself:

- When do I feel most alive, grounded, and proud of myself?
- What kind of life would make me feel at peace—even if no one else saw it or applauded it?

Step 3: Ego vs. Soul Check-In

For each statement below, choose what feels most true for *you* right now:

Prompt	Ego's Answer	Soul's Answer
I feel successful when...	_____	_____
I feel happy when...	_____	_____
I feel confident when...	_____	_____
I make decisions based on...	_____	_____

Step 4: Shift the Focus

What's one small change you can make this week to move from ego-led living to aligned living?

Example: "Instead of overworking to prove I'm enough, I'll rest because I know I'm worthy either way."

Final Thoughts: The Power of Letting Go and Living Fully

You don't need ego to be powerful.

You don't need to prove yourself to be worthy.

You don't need external validation to be happy.

The most powerful people in the world? **They don't live for their ego—they live for their purpose.**

And now? **So do you.**

Because once you master ego, you step into:

A life of clarity, not confusion.

A life of wisdom, not reaction.

A life where you're free to be your best self—without limits.

This is the ultimate freedom. And it's yours.

Chapter 21: How Ego Creates Generational Trauma
(And How to Break the Cycle From the Parent's Perspective)

Ego isn't just personal—it's inherited. Passed down in the way we speak, the way we love, the way we protect, and sometimes... the way we hurt. It shapes how families communicate, how emotions are handled, and how love is expressed—or withheld.

Most parents truly want their children to have a better life than they did. But sometimes, when that wish becomes reality, the ego feels threatened.

Instead of feeling proud, ego turns their child's ease into a trigger.

"I struggled—why don't you have to?"

"Back in my day, we didn't complain about things like that."

"You don't know what real hardship is."

And just like that, pain becomes competition.

Resentment replaces connection.

And progress is dismissed as weakness.

This is how generational trauma begins—not always through abuse or neglect, but through ego-driven expectations, emotional invalidation, and a refusal to see the child as their own person, with their own experiences.

Instead of learning from each other, families become stuck in cycles of unspoken wounds, defensive pride, and emotional distance.

Parents feel disrespected.

Children feel misunderstood.

And love becomes conditional—based on obedience, sacrifice, or suffering.

This chapter is about recognizing how ego fuels that cycle—and how to break it.

Whether you're a parent, the child of one, or both... this is an invitation to create something different. Something healthier. Something healing.

Because breaking the cycle doesn't mean dishonoring the past. It means honoring yourself *enough* to do things better.

1. Struggle Becomes an Identity

For many parents, suffering wasn't a phase—it was their entire reality.

Not by choice, but by circumstance.

They had to work as children, not because they wanted to, but because survival required it.

They had no safe space to express emotions—crying was weakness, and needing support was "being dramatic." They weren't taught to heal. They were taught to *cope*—quietly, and alone.

So what happens when that kind of pain never gets processed?

Ego steps in to protect the wound. And instead of releasing the struggle, they start *identifying* with it. They wear their pain like a badge of honor.

Not just, "I struggled."

But:

"I struggled, so you don't have a right to feel what you feel."
"I struggled, so your pain doesn't count unless it looks like mine."
"I struggled, and if you don't, it means I was weak for going through it."

And the unspoken belief becomes:

"If life was hard for me, it should be hard for you, too."

This is how trauma gets passed down—not just through what happened, but through the mindset that suffering is required for growth, worth, or respect.

Instead of being proud that their child has it easier, ego makes it feel unfair.

Instead of breaking the cycle, it starts repeating itself in subtle, emotional ways:

Children feel guilty for having more ease.

They start shrinking their joy, their emotions, their needs—to avoid seeming "ungrateful."

And eventually, they internalize the message: *"My pain only matters if I earn it."*

But trauma doesn't only live in what happened—it also lives in what was *invalidated.*

And when struggle becomes a source of pride instead of something to heal, ego becomes the chain that keeps the pain alive.

The cycle continues—not because parents don't love their children, but because their ego hasn't been taught the difference between survival and healing.

2. Success Feels Like an Insult

When a parent grows up in survival mode, and their child grows up in stability, ego can twist that into something ugly. Instead of seeing their child's comfort as a sign of progress, it starts to feel like a personal attack.

"I had to fight for everything I have. Why do you get it so easy?"

"You'll never understand real hardship."

"You kids are soft."

Instead of feeling proud that their child doesn't have to suffer, they feel *offended* by it.

Instead of celebrating the fact that they broke the cycle... they start resenting the fact that their child never had to *survive* like they did.

Ego whispers: *"If they didn't struggle like me, their life has no meaning."*

"If it came easier for them, they must be spoiled, ungrateful, or weak."

"If they didn't earn it through pain, they don't deserve it."

But that couldn't be further from the truth.

The entire point of generational growth is that the next generation doesn't have to struggle the same way.

The goal was never to pass the pain down—it was to rise above it.

What looks like "ease" to the ego is actually the evidence of healing.

It means the sacrifice wasn't for nothing.

It means something changed.

It means the fight worked.

But when pain becomes identity, watching someone live without it can feel threatening.

It can make parents feel unseen, invalidated, or forgotten—like their suffering is being erased or minimized.

So instead of saying, *"I'm proud of you,"* the ego says, *"You don't appreciate how hard it was for me."*

That's when resentment replaces love. And the child, instead of feeling supported, starts feeling guilty for having what their parent never did.

They shrink their joy.

They minimize their success.

They carry shame for being the product of their parent's hard work—because instead of being celebrated, they're made to feel ungrateful for not suffering the same way.

But let's be clear:

Breaking generational struggle was always the point.

You didn't work hard just to pass on your pain.

You worked hard so they *wouldn't* have to.

The most powerful legacy isn't survival—it's peace. And choosing to celebrate your child's success, instead of resenting it, is how you *truly* break the cycle.

3. Emotional Invalidation Becomes the Norm

When parents believe their own struggles were harder, they start to measure everything against their pain—and anything "less" doesn't count.

"You're stressed? About what? You don't even pay bills."

"You're depressed? You have food, a roof, and clothes—you should be grateful."

"You think that's hard? Back in my day..."

Instead of listening, they compare.

Instead of empathizing, they downplay.

Instead of creating emotional safety, they create emotional shame.

And here's what that teaches kids:

"My problems don't matter."

So they stop opening up. They suppress everything. They learn to self-abandon just to avoid being judged.

"I have to prove my pain to be taken seriously."

So they start chasing struggle, making things harder than they need to be—because suffering becomes the only way to feel *seen*.

And just like that, the cycle continues.

Ego doesn't just invalidate—it *grades* pain. It plays the "who had it worse" game, as if emotional suffering has to meet a certain threshold to be real.

And we do this more than we realize.

Not just with people, but even with pets.

People say things like:

"What's he stressed about? He's a dog. He sleeps all day."

As if *rest* means *absence of emotion*. As if *lack of responsibilities* means *lack of experience*.

We invalidate animals, children, and even our younger selves—forgetting that emotions don't follow logic.

You don't need to have bills to feel anxious.

You don't need to have trauma to feel pain. You don't need to be a human with a full-time job to feel overwhelmed.

Pain is *relative.*

And when someone is expressing it, they're not asking you to compare—they're asking you to care.

The moment we stop measuring pain and start *witnessing* it, healing begins.

Because no matter the size of the problem, *feeling heard* is what so many people—and kids—are truly starving for.

4. Authority Becomes More Important Than Connection

In many households, **respect** is often confused with **obedience.** Ego teaches parents that being "in charge" matters more than being *in tune.*

So instead of nurturing connection, they enforce control.

"I'm the parent, you're the child—I don't have to explain myself."

"I've lived longer than you, so I know better."

"Talking back" = Any attempt to express yourself, even if it's calm, valid, or honest.

And just like that, the opportunity for a real relationship is replaced with a one-sided power dynamic. Instead of creating emotional safety, ego demands compliance. Instead of encouraging growth, ego demands silence.

But here's what gets forgotten:

Your child is not just an extension of your authority. They're their own person—with thoughts, feelings, and a voice that deserves to be heard.

When children are constantly shut down or punished for expressing themselves, they eventually stop trying.

They learn that honesty = disrespect.

That vulnerability = rebellion.

That having emotions = being "too sensitive" or "out of line."

So they go quiet.

Not out of peace—but out of *self-protection*.

And that silence doesn't build closeness. It builds resentment, emotional distance, and a lifelong struggle to speak up.

Generational disconnect doesn't always begin with abuse. Sometimes, it begins with good intentions delivered through the lens of ego—where being right is more important than being open.

True leadership, especially as a parent, isn't about control—it's about *connection*

How to Break the Cycle

Mastering ego isn't just personal—it's *generational*. It's about healing the pain you inherited so you don't pass it down. It's about choosing to respond with love, even when your ego wants to react with pride.

And most of all, it's about stopping the trauma *before* it repeats.

Here's how you begin:

1. Recognize That Struggle Doesn't Equal Worth

Just because you suffered doesn't mean your child has to. Just because their struggles look different doesn't mean they're not real.

266

Just because you worked harder doesn't mean they don't deserve ease.

Breaking the cycle means celebrating their freedom—not resenting it. It means realizing that your child having more is not a reflection of you being weak—it's a reflection of your strength. You made life easier for them. That's not failure. That's *progress.*

2. Stop Competing With Your Child's Experience

"You think you have it hard? When I was your age…"

"I had to do everything on my own—so should you."

"I survived without therapy, so why do you need it?"

Your child's needs are not an attack on your past.

They're not calling you a bad parent.

They're just asking to be seen, heard, and supported in *their* reality.

Instead of defending your experience, *lean into theirs.* Ask:

"What are you struggling with right now?"

"How can I support you through it?"

"What do you need from me, even if I don't fully understand?"

That's not weakness. That's wisdom.

3. Shift from Authority to Understanding

Being older doesn't automatically mean you're right. Respect shouldn't be demanded through fear—it's earned through compassion.

Your child isn't here to fulfill your expectations. They're here to become themselves.

They don't need to be *controlled*. They need to be *understood*.

Try saying:

"I may not relate to your struggles, but I'm open to hearing them."

"Tell me how you feel—even if I don't agree, I care enough to listen."

"You're my child, yes—but you're also a whole human being."

When ego steps aside, connection takes its place. When power stops being the goal, love becomes the language. And when you lead with curiosity instead of control, the healing begins.

Exercise: Breaking the Cycle with Awareness & Intention

A Reflection for Healing Generational Ego

This isn't about blame—it's about awareness. This isn't about shame—it's about *change*.

Use this exercise to gently explore the patterns you were raised with, how they may be showing up now, and how you can choose differently moving forward.

Step 1: What Were You Taught?

Growing up, what messages did you receive about struggle, emotions, and respect?

- When I struggled as a child, I was told:
- When I expressed emotion, the response was:
- I was expected to show respect by:

Step 2: What Did You *Need* Instead?

Now reflect on what would have helped you feel seen, supported, or safe:

- I needed someone to say:
- I needed space to feel:
- I needed less _____ and more _____:

Step 3: What Are You Passing Down (Consciously or Unconsciously)?

Get honest with yourself—no judgment, just clarity:

One way ego may show up in my parenting or relationships:

A moment I dismissed someone's emotions because they didn't match my experience:

Something I say out of pride that might be hurting connection:

Step 4: What Do You Want to Do Differently?

This is where healing begins—through intention.

- One belief I want to release:
- One new way I'll respond when someone opens up to me:
- One reminder I'll carry with me when ego wants to take over:

Example: "Their emotions don't invalidate my experience—we can both be human at the same time."

Optional Affirmation to End With:

"I am not here to repeat the pain I was handed. I am here to heal it, understand it, and do better—with love, not ego."

Final Thoughts: Generational Healing Starts With You

Ego convinces parents that **being right is more important than being present.**

Ego convinces kids that **their voices don't matter.**

But breaking the cycle means **choosing connection over control.**

It means listening.

It means validating emotions—even when you don't relate.

It means realizing that progress isn't a competition—it's a blessing.

Because at the end of the day, **the real flex isn't passing down pain.**

The real flex is **healing, evolving, and building a future where struggle is no longer the only measure of success.**

Chapter 22: Breaking the Cycle from the Child's Perspective
(When Your Parents Won't Do the Work, You Have to Do It Yourself)

Not every parent wants to break the cycle. Some are too stuck in their ways—too wrapped up in pride, ego, and a rigid definition of "respect" to ever admit they might have caused harm.

To them, parenting means control, not connection. And accountability? That feels like disrespect.

So what happens when your pain is met with denial? When your truth is silenced with guilt?

When the people who were supposed to protect you are the ones you now have to protect *yourself* from?

You're left with two choices:

1. Repeat the cycle.

Become just like them.

Let the pain harden you.

Use their words. Copy their silence. Invalidate others the way you were invalidated.

Let ego tell you, *"This is just how I was raised."* And keep the trauma alive—passing it down like a family tradition.

2. Break the cycle.

Do the work they refused to do.

Feel what they avoided.

Heal what they ignored.

Become the kind of person you needed—especially for your own future, your relationships, your peace.

Option 1 is easier.

All it takes is silence.

You just keep the resentment, absorb the dysfunction, and pass it on.

Option 2? That's the hard path.

It takes strength, vulnerability, patience, and grace.

It means grieving the version of your parents you'll never have. It means learning to give yourself the love, validation, and support they couldn't—or wouldn't—give.

But it also means *freedom*.

It means peace.

It means building a life that feels safe, intentional, and whole— not in spite of your past, but because you *chose* not to let it define you.

This chapter is for every person who had to become their own healer.

For the ones who never got an apology.

For the ones who were told to "just get over it."

For the ones breaking the cycle *with no roadmap*.

You didn't choose the pain.

But you get to choose what happens next.

Let's talk about how to do that.

1. Accept That They May Never Change

One of the hardest truths to accept is that not every parent is willing—or capable—of doing the work.

You can't force self-awareness onto someone who isn't ready for it.

You can't heal someone who refuses to admit they've hurt you.

And you don't need their understanding or approval to move forward.

If they still:

- Dismiss your emotions with phrases like, "You're too sensitive."
- Avoid accountability by saying, "I did the best I could—stop blaming me."
- Make your healing about their ego with lines like, "I went through worse, and you don't see me complaining."

Then it's time to stop searching for closure in places that continue to reopen the wound.

Some parents will never say:

- "I'm sorry."
- "I was wrong."
- "I should have been better."

And that's painful.

It's a grief most people never talk about—the loss of the parent you *wish* you had while still having to interact with the one you do. But waiting for them to become who you needed is what keeps you stuck.

You don't have to wait for their apology to begin your healing. You don't have to stay in emotional limbo hoping they'll suddenly understand.

Letting go doesn't mean you're okay with what happened. It means you're no longer allowing it to define your worth or your future.

This is your permission to move forward—even if they never do.

2. Stop Seeking Validation from Them

If your parents were emotionally unavailable, dismissive, or only supportive when it suited them, then deep down, you may have never felt "good enough" in their eyes.

And that feeling doesn't just fade with age—it lingers.

You keep trying to earn what should have been freely given.

You keep waiting for the version of them that never showed up.

Why? Because their love was conditional.

- You had to be successful enough to earn praise.
- You had to behave enough to be respected.
- You had to struggle enough to be taken seriously.

So now, even as an adult, you might find yourself still waiting...

Waiting for them to finally say they're proud of you. Waiting for them to admit your pain was real. Waiting for them to respect your choices, your truth, your healing— *you*.

But here's the truth:

You don't need their validation anymore. You don't need to keep shrinking yourself, exhausting yourself, or bending over backwards for approval that's tied to their ego, not your worth.

- You are worthy, whether they see it or not.
- Your emotions are valid, whether they understand them or not.
- Your growth is real, even if they never acknowledge it.

Let go of the need to be seen by people who only know how to love through control.

You don't have to keep proving your value to someone who was supposed to nurture it from the start.

Your healing is not dependent on their awakening. You get to choose yourself—even if they never chose to see you clearly.

3. Set Boundaries Without Guilt

Some parents try to guilt their children into silence, submission, or emotional exhaustion by hiding behind the weight of what they've done.

They might say things like:

- "You owe me for everything I did for you."
- "You wouldn't be here without me."
- "I raised you, so you have to respect me."

But here's the truth:

Love without boundaries is not love—it's control. And respect should go *both* ways.

You are allowed to:

- Say no without explaining yourself.
- Distance yourself from people who drain, dismiss, or disrespect you—even if they're family.
- Prioritize your mental and emotional health over their unspoken rules and outdated expectations.

Because your peace is not up for negotiation.

Setting boundaries doesn't make you disrespectful.

It doesn't make you selfish or ungrateful.

It means you love yourself enough to protect your energy—even from those who helped shape your world.

Let this be your reminder:

- A boundary is not disconnection. It's clarity.
- A boundary is not punishment. It's protection.
- A boundary is not disrespect. It's *self-respect*.

And if they can't respect that?

That's not your burden to carry.

It's theirs to confront.

4. Process the Hurt Without Becoming Them

When you grow up with emotionally unavailable, dismissive, or controlling parents, it's easy to carry those wounds into adulthood—and even easier to repeat the same patterns without realizing it.

You might:

- Struggle to express emotions because you were taught to suppress them.

- Have trouble receiving love because you were conditioned to believe you had to *earn* it.
- Feel deep anger toward your parents—and end up projecting it onto the people closest to you.

This isn't because you're broken. It's because unhealed pain has a way of leaking into your present.

But here's the key:

You don't have to become what hurt you.

Breaking the cycle means doing the opposite of what ego tells you to do.

It means *feeling* instead of numbing.

Reflecting instead of reacting.

Rewriting instead of repeating.

Breaking the cycle means:

- Learning to communicate instead of shutting down.
- Letting yourself be loved without trying to earn it.
- Healing your anger without letting it become your identity.
- Showing up as the parent, partner, friend—or *human*— that you needed when you were younger.

Because even if your pain wasn't your fault, your healing *is* your responsibility.

You can't change what they did.

You can't force them to apologize, evolve, or understand.

But you can stop the pattern with *you*.

And that alone?

That's powerful. That's generational healing. That's freedom.

5. Build a Life That Isn't Defined by Your Pain

You are not doomed to live out the same emotional script you were handed.

You are not obligated to carry someone else's wounds just because they refused to heal them.

And you are not required to stay small, angry, or broken just because that's the energy you grew up around.

- You don't have to stay stuck in the mindset you were raised in.
- You don't have to inherit their bitterness, fear, or emotional walls.
- You don't have to live in the shadow of their expectations—or their regrets.

At some point, you have to make a decision: Will your life be a reaction to your pain... or a reflection of your *power*?

Because the truth is:

- Your childhood may explain you—but it does *not* define you.
- Your parents may have shaped your early years—but they don't own your future.
- You are not their mistakes. You are not their projections. You are not the pain they refused to face.

You are your own person. And that means you get to choose who you become.

The moment you stop waiting for them to change, the moment you stop making your healing about *them*—that's the moment you step into freedom.

A new chapter begins the second you say: **"This ends with me."**

Exercise: Who Are You *Without* the Pain?

This exercise is about separating your *truth* from your *trauma*. It's about asking: "Who am I when I'm not trying to survive what they did to me?"

Let's go there—with compassion, honesty, and intention.

Step 1: Acknowledge What You Inherited

What emotional patterns, beliefs, or fears did you absorb growing   up?
Complete the statements below:

- I was taught that love means:
- I was made to feel like I had to:
- I still catch myself believing:

Step 2: Release the Shadow

What parts of your identity are rooted in defense or survival—not choice?

- I act this way because I'm still protecting myself from:
- I've been defining myself by:
- But I know now... that's not who I really am.

Step 3: Redefine Yourself

Now, without reference to your pain, your parents, or your past—who are you?

- I am someone who:
- I value:
- I feel most alive when:
- I am becoming:

Step 4: Your New Standard

Complete this sentence as a declaration to yourself:

"I no longer live in reaction to my pain. I live in alignment with my purpose."

Or write your own.

Step 5: Reclaim Something You Were Told Not to Do

Is there something you wanted to try—something creative, expressive, adventurous, or just *you*—but didn't?

Maybe it was an activity.

A passion.

A dream.

Or a part of your personality you held back because someone said it was "too much," "too risky," or "not for you."

Sometimes parents say no out of fear or protection. They want to keep you safe, and what feels unfamiliar to them can seem dangerous or unrealistic.

Other times, it comes out more harshly—through criticism, judgment, or control.

No matter where it came from, the impact can be the same:

280

You learn to play small.

You hesitate.

You hold yourself back—even long after you're grown.

But part of breaking the cycle means asking:

- **What did I stop myself from doing because someone else couldn't see it for me?**
- **What's something you've always wanted to try—but avoided because of someone else's fear, doubt, or judgment?**
- **What's one small way you could give yourself *permission* to try it now—just for you?**

This isn't about blame—it's about becoming.

You're not rejecting where you came from.

You're reconnecting with the parts of yourself that never got to shine.

Bonus Reflection Questions:

What do you think that version of you—the one who wanted to try—needed to hear at the time?

Maybe it was: *"It's okay to explore."*

Or: *"You don't need to be perfect to begin."*

Or even just: *"I believe in you."*

How would it feel to give that version of you a second chance—right now?

Healing isn't always about fixing the past. Sometimes, it's about doing the thing anyway—and proving to yourself that it was always safe to want more.

Final Thoughts: You Are Not Your Parents' Pain— You Are Your Own Healing

Not every parent will do the work.

Not every parent will understand you.

Not every parent will see you as a person instead of just "their child."

But **your healing does not require their approval.**

You have two choices:

1. Repeat the cycle.

2. Break it and build something better.

And if you're reading this, you already know which one you're choosing.

Because **you're not just healing for yourself—you're healing for the generations that come after you.**

You are the cycle breaker.

And that? **That's the real legacy.**

Part 6: The Bigger Picture

Ego's True Impact on Your Life — and Your Power to Rise Above It

At this point, you've seen it all.

The subtle masks. The loud defenses. The quiet sabotage. The need to control, prove, protect, and perform.

Ego isn't just a one-time mistake — it's a pattern. A lens. A filter that warps how you see yourself, how you treat others, and how you move through the world. And if you're not conscious of it? It *runs your entire life* while convincing you that you're in control.

But now, the awareness is here.

You've learned how ego hides. How it speaks. How it deflects. And most importantly — how to recognize it before it runs the show.

This final section isn't about being perfect. It's about *power.*

The power to choose something better.

To rise above fear.

To stop reacting and start responding.

To live from truth — not pride. From purpose — not performance.

You vs. ego.

Who wins?

That choice is yours now.

Let's step into the bigger picture.

Chapter 23: Ego the Silent Killer

Ego is a **silent killer** of so many things beyond generational trauma—it keeps people trapped in toxic cycles without even realizing it.

Here are some **major life issues** caused by ego:

1. Broken Relationships & Family Estrangement

Ego can destroy relationships that were never supposed to end.

It convinces people that being *right* is more important than being *connected.* That pride matters more than peace. And instead of healing, people hold grudges. Instead of talking, they stay silent. Instead of reaching out, they assume the worst—and let the relationship die in the dark.

You see it everywhere:

- Sibling rivalries that linger for years because no one wants to be the one to say, *"I miss you."*
- Parents who can't accept their child's truth because they feel "disrespected," confusing control with care.
- Friendships that fall apart over misunderstandings, because both sides would rather protect their ego than repair the bond.

And just like that, love gets buried under layers of unspoken pain.

Ego keeps people bitter instead of healing.

It creates this toxic chain reaction:

Something painful happens → No one wants to admit fault → Time passes → Ego hardens → Everyone assumes the other person doesn't care → The relationship fades into silence.

And the saddest part?

Most of these connections could've been repaired. But ego made the silence feel safer than vulnerability.

How to Break It

- Apologize, even if you weren't the "worst" one.
- Let go of needing to be *right* in order to be real.
- Extend grace, even if you never received it.
- Be the one who chooses *peace* over *pride*.

Reconnection doesn't always mean reunion. Sometimes it just means releasing the bitterness in your heart—so it doesn't grow roots and become part of your identity.

Not every relationship can (or should) be restored. But if there's still love underneath the silence? Let that matter more than your ego.

2. Financial Struggles & Stagnation

Ego can keep you broke—not because you're incapable, but because it convinces you that humbling yourself is a threat instead of a stepping stone.

Instead of starting where they are, people get stuck trying to protect an image.

They'd rather *look* successful than *be* stable. They avoid the basics—saving, budgeting, asking questions—because ego sees those things as weakness.

You see it all the time:

- People turning down honest work because it doesn't match the lifestyle they want to project.
- Avoiding financial literacy because they don't want to admit they were never taught how money works.
- Spending money they don't have to maintain an aesthetic—cars, clothes, vacations—just to avoid feeling "less than."

Ego makes people feel "too good" to start at the bottom, but not too good to stay stuck.

The Cycle Looks Like This:

Fear of looking "broke" → Bad financial decisions → No savings → Bigger struggles later → Blame placed on external factors (the economy, other people, bad luck)... instead of examining ego.

It's not that people don't want financial freedom. It's that ego convinces them they should *already* have it—and if they don't, something must be wrong with them. So they overcompensate instead of learning.

But the truth is: **you're not "less than" because you're starting small.**

You're only stuck if you refuse to begin.

How to Break It

- Learn the skills you were never taught—budgeting, credit, investing, saving.
- Ask for help from someone who knows more—without shame.
- Stop trying to prove you're "already there" and focus on actually *getting there.*
- Build slow. Grow smart. Choose long-term peace over short-term flexing.

Because real wealth isn't loud.

It's quiet.

It's consistent.

And it starts when ego steps aside—and discipline steps in.

3. Toxic Work Environments & Career Stagnation

Ego doesn't just damage relationships—it destroys growth. Especially in your career.

When ego is in control, people stop learning. They stop listening.

They become so attached to *being right* or *being in charge* that they miss opportunities to actually get *better.*

And it shows:

- The coworker who acts like they know everything—and shuts down when challenged.
- The manager who micromanages every detail because deep down, they don't trust anyone but themselves.

- The business owner who refuses to evolve—stuck in the same outdated habits because "this has always worked."

Ego makes people mistake authority for wisdom—and confidence for control.

But in reality, ego is often what's keeping them from leveling up.

The Cycle Looks Like This:

Believes they know best → Rejects feedback → Stagnates professionally → Feels overlooked or frustrated → Blames the system, coworkers, or circumstances—never themselves → Stays stuck.

Meanwhile, people with less experience but more humility?

They're growing.

They're adapting.

They're moving forward while ego keeps others in place.

And here's the truth:

You don't rise by acting like you've already arrived.

You grow by staying open.

How to Break It

- Stay a student—even when you're a leader.
- Be coachable. The most successful people *want* feedback because they're committed to growth.
- Don't let your title or experience block your curiosity.
- Stay humble enough to try something new—even if you've "been doing this for years."

Because in any career or calling, ego is the ceiling. Letting it go? That's what breaks the limits.

4. Failed Romantic Relationships & Divorce

Ego can't love—it can only compete.

When ego takes over in relationships, love becomes a power struggle.

Everything turns into a win-or-lose scenario. And instead of building a partnership, people build walls.

It shows up in ways that feel small at first:

- A partner who refuses to say "I'm sorry" because they think it makes them weak.
- Someone who picks fights not to resolve—but to *win*.
- Two people who love each other deeply... but let their pride speak louder than their hearts.

Over time, ego poisons the connection. The relationship becomes less about *us* and more about *me vs. you*.

Ego convinces people that being right is more important than being together.

That proving a point matters more than protecting the bond. And slowly, resentment replaces intimacy.

The Cycle Looks Like This:

Ego-driven fights → No one takes accountability → Grudges build → Communication fades → Emotional walls go up → Breakup or divorce over things that could've been healed—if ego hadn't been in the way.

So many relationships don't fail because of lack of love. They fail because of *too much ego and not enough humility.*

How to Break It

- Let go of needing to win every argument.
- Apologize sincerely—without defensiveness or blame-shifting.
- Choose listening over reacting.
- Ask yourself in moments of tension: *"Do I want to be right... or do I want to be close?"*

Because love isn't a debate.

It's a commitment to keep coming back to each other—even when it's hard, even when it's messy.

And the moment ego steps aside, connection can finally step in.

5. Losing Opportunities Because of Arrogance

Sometimes, the biggest thing standing between you and the life you want...

is the belief that you already know everything.

Ego makes people overestimate their abilities—and underestimate what it takes to grow.

It convinces them that preparation is unnecessary, help is weakness, and new opportunities are beneath them.

You see it in real time:

- Someone walking into a big interview unprepared because they assume charm alone will carry them.

- Someone refusing to network, collaborate, or learn from others because they believe, *"I don't need anyone."*
- Someone dismissing a potential opportunity because it's not flashy, not "their vibe," or doesn't fit their ego's version of success.

Ego tells you, "You're already good enough."

And yes—you *are* enough.

But that doesn't mean you're done growing.

The Cycle Looks Like This:

Overconfidence → Lack of preparation or effort → Missed opportunity → Frustration and blame → Repeats the same behavior without reflection → Stays stuck while others pass them by.

It's not that these people don't have talent. It's that their *ego* keeps them from putting in the work that would *maximize* that talent.

Opportunities don't wait for ego to catch up. They favor the prepared, the humble, and the open-minded.

How to Break It

- Stay humble—even when you're confident.
- Be willing to start at the bottom, even when you know you have potential.
- Stay open to learning from people with different experiences, styles, and perspectives.
- Ask more questions. Listen more than you speak. Prepare like it's your first time, every time.

Because ego might make you feel powerful for a moment... but humility is what unlocks the doors ego will never even knock on.

6. Inherited Cultural & Gender-Based Toxicity

Ego isn't always personal—it's often *programmed.*

From a young age, we're taught what it means to "be a man" or "be a woman."

We're handed roles, expectations, and unspoken rules based on culture, gender, tradition, and pride.

And most of the time?

No one questions if those rules actually make sense.

- Men are taught that showing emotion is weakness— because *"real men don't cry."*

- Women are taught to silence themselves, toughen up, or "act like a lady"—because *"being soft is being weak."*

- People across all identities are told to fit in, shrink down, and follow the roles assigned to them—even when it's hurting them.

Ego shows up here as pride in tradition, even when the tradition is toxic.

It says, "This is just how it is," instead of asking, "But is this actually healthy?"

The Cycle Looks Like This:

Society hands down toxic beliefs → People internalize them without reflection → They act them out and pass them down →

Generations continue to suffer in silence—believing that anything different is "wrong," "soft," or "dangerous."

It's not always malicious—it's often subconscious. But that doesn't make the impact any less damaging.

And if no one questions it, the cycle *never* breaks.

How to Break It

- Question the beliefs you were raised with. Not to disrespect your culture or your roots—but to *heal* what never should've been normalized.
- Embrace emotional intelligence. Vulnerability doesn't make you weak—it makes you *free*.
- Redefine what strength really means. Sometimes strength is speaking up. Sometimes it's walking away. Sometimes it's *letting yourself feel*.

Strength isn't gendered.

Wisdom isn't cultural.

And healing isn't rebellion—it's *evolution*.

7. Stagnant Personal Growth & Unfulfilled Potential

Ego doesn't just make people loud—it makes them *stuck*.

It whispers, *"You're already good enough."*

But instead of that being a statement of self-worth, it becomes an excuse to stop evolving.

Growth gets replaced with defensiveness.

Curiosity turns into complacency.

And slowly, ego convinces people that staying the same is safer than leveling up.

You see it everywhere:

- People who refuse to read, learn, or grow because they think, *"I already know what I need to know."*
- People who avoid therapy or self-reflection because they associate needing help with being broken.
- People who instantly shut down when offered feedback—because to them, being corrected feels like being judged.

But the truth is: **ego doesn't protect your confidence—it protects your comfort.**

And comfort zones are where potential goes to die.

The Cycle Looks Like This:

Avoids growth → Stays the same → Blames others or life for feeling stuck → Resists all forms of change → Misses the transformation they were capable of.

The worst part?

Sometimes the people with the most talent, wisdom, or promise stay small—because ego convinced them there was nothing left to learn.

But growth isn't about proving you're not good enough. It's about honoring the fact that you're capable of *even more.*

How to Break It

- Stay hungry for knowledge. Read, ask questions, challenge your own beliefs.
- Embrace self-reflection. The most powerful people are the ones who *know themselves.*
- Stay open to discomfort. Growth is messy. It's vulnerable. It's uncomfortable. But that's where the magic happens.

Your life can't expand if your mindset doesn't. And your purpose can't unfold if your ego refuses to evolve.

Humility isn't weakness—it's the foundation of *real* confidence.

Exercise: Who Could You Be Without Ego Holding You Back?

This isn't about tearing yourself down.

It's about getting radically honest—with love.

Because ego may protect your pride, but it also blocks your growth.

Let's find out where you're holding yourself back... and how to move forward.

Step 1: Where Have You Stopped Growing?

- What area of your life feels "stuck" right now?
- What story have you been telling yourself about why you can't grow here?

- Be honest: Is it fear, pride, or ego that's keeping you from changing this?

Step 2: What Would Growth Look Like If Ego Wasn't in the Way?

- If I wasn't afraid of being wrong or judged, I would:
- If I didn't need to "look like I have it all together," I'd try:
- If I truly believed growth was strength, not failure, I would:

Step 3: Visualize Your Next-Level Self

Imagine the version of you who chose *growth* over *ego*.

- What habits do they have?
- How do they respond to feedback or challenges?
- What kind of peace, purpose, or power do they have that you're still working toward?

Affirmation to Close:

"I release the need to protect an outdated version of myself.

I give myself permission to evolve—loudly, quietly, painfully, beautifully.

I don't need to stay the same to prove I'm enough. I grow because I'm ready."

Final Thoughts: Ego Is the Root of So Many Issues

When you zoom out and really look at the patterns—the broken bonds, the cycles of pain, the missed chances—you'll notice one thing:

Ego is always in the middle.

- Broken families? Ego made people choose pride over connection.
- Financial struggles? Ego kept people too proud to start small or ask for help.
- Relationship failures? Ego turned love into a power struggle.
- Missed opportunities? Ego said, *"You're above this,"* and let the moment slip away.

Ego isn't always loud. Sometimes it's quiet. It hides behind fear, control, avoidance, perfectionism, and pride. And the worst part? Most people don't even realize it's ego that's holding them back.

They blame everything else—everyone else—without ever looking inward.

But here's the truth:

- **Master ego, and you master your life.**
- **Kill ego, and you break generational cycles that have lived in your bloodline for decades.**
- **Control ego, and you walk through doors most people will never even see—because their pride keeps them blind.**

Ego is either your biggest enemy...
or your greatest teacher.

And the power to choose?

It's always been yours.

Chapter 24: The Rise of the Real You (The version of you that doesn't need to prove anything)

This isn't about becoming someone new. It's about finally *being* who you were underneath all the noise.

The real you isn't chasing approval.
It isn't tied to productivity, perfection, or needing to be understood.
It doesn't perform for acceptance or shrink for comfort.

The real you knows you're enough — and moves like it.

And the moment you stop living through the lens of ego is the moment everything shifts.

You don't stop caring — you just stop *needing* validation to feel secure.

You don't stop showing up — you just stop over-explaining your worth to people who were never listening.

What Actually Happens When the Ego Drops

Let's make it plain — when ego isn't running the show anymore, everything shifts.

Not just how you act, but how you think, how you feel, and how you move.

You stop making decisions out of fear — and start making them from alignment.

No more choices rooted in insecurity, scarcity, or the fear of being judged.

You start asking: "Does this feel right for me?" instead of "Will they approve?"

Your intuition leads — not your survival mode.

You stop rushing to fix your image — and start focusing on your integrity.

You're not scrambling to control how you look to others.

Instead, you make sure your actions reflect who you really are — even if no one's watching.

You care more about being honest than looking perfect.
You'd rather be real than polished.

You stop managing how people see you — and start managing how you feel around them.

It's no longer about keeping up appearances — it's about keeping your peace.

You start asking yourself: "Do I feel safe, seen, and respected in this space?"

Because it's not about being liked by everyone — it's about being loved by the right ones, starting with yourself.

You stop trying to prove your value — and start embodying it.

You no longer need external validation to feel worthy.

You know who you are, and that confidence radiates quietly.

You don't announce your growth — you live it.

You become undeniable without needing to be loud.

You're no longer consumed with looking impressive — you're more interested in being at peace.

Success stops being a performance.

You stop chasing aesthetics and start pursuing authenticity.

Peace becomes the goal — not perfection.

You stop reacting to every trigger — not because you're passive, but because you've developed the power to pause, reflect, and choose your response.

You're not ignoring your emotions — you're mastering them.

You're not suppressing — you're redirecting.

You don't need to clap back or explain yourself every time — because silence is no longer uncomfortable. It's intentional.

That's what the real you sounds like.

Not louder — **clearer.**

Not harder — **deeper.**

Not perfect — **present.**

And when the noise of ego fades, you don't lose your power — you remember where it actually lives.

Letting Go of Ego to Step Into Your Higher Self

Your higher self isn't perfect — it's just *present.* It doesn't need to prove anything because it's rooted in truth.

It knows that being wrong doesn't make you unworthy.

That rest isn't laziness.

That silence is a strength.

That peace is more valuable than being "right."

When ego fades, *you don't disappear — you arrive.* Fully. Finally.

You trust your own voice more than outside opinions.

You lead from intention, not insecurity.

And you no longer feel the need to *keep up* — because you're already in alignment with who you were always meant to be.

The Real You in Action

Let's be clear — the version of you that's no longer run by ego doesn't just *think* differently... you *move* differently.

You don't just talk about healing — you embody it.

You don't just know your worth — you live like it.

And that shows up in *every area* of your life:

In relationships:

You stop over-giving just to feel wanted.

You no longer pour into people hoping they'll choose you back.

You don't romanticize breadcrumbs or make excuses for half-effort energy.

You show up as someone who is whole, secure, and rooted — and you expect the same.

Love becomes mutual, not performative.

You're not afraid to walk away from what doesn't honor your softness, your truth, or your capacity.

In your work:

You stop performing for applause and start working from purpose.

You stop burning yourself out trying to prove you're capable.

You recognize that your worth isn't tied to your productivity, your title, or your to-do list.

You no longer chase goals that impress others — you pursue the ones that fulfill *you*.

You're not working to be enough. You're creating from a place of *already being enough*.

In your self-talk:

You stop tearing yourself apart every time you fall short.

You stop bullying yourself in the name of "self-discipline."

You start speaking to yourself with the same grace, patience, and compassion you give others.

You don't shame your humanity — you hold it.

You become your own safe space, your own hype person, your own anchor.

Not perfectly. Not always. But consistently enough to notice the shift.

In your boundaries:

You don't set boundaries to punish. You set them to protect.

You no longer over-explain or beg for understanding.

You say what you need and let it stand.

You stop confusing guilt with responsibility.

You recognize that you don't owe anyone access to your energy just because they used to have it.

Your peace becomes the priority — not the performance of being "nice."

In your presence:

You walk into rooms with clarity — not insecurity.

You're not scanning the room for approval. You're sensing the energy, the fit, the alignment.

You don't need everyone to like you — you just need to feel like *yourself* wherever you are.

You take up space with quiet confidence, because you're no longer shrinking to be accepted or inflating to be admired.

You're just *being*. And that's enough.

This isn't about ego death — it's about ego *balance*. You're not trying to erase your ego. You're just not letting it lead. You're not silencing it to disappear — you're silencing it so the **real you** can finally be heard.

The real you isn't fighting to be seen anymore — Because now, you *see yourself*.

The Joy of Living Unbothered, Self-Assured, and Free

This version of you doesn't need applause to feel accomplished.

Doesn't need comparison to feel confident.

Doesn't need chaos to feel alive.

It doesn't mean life gets easier — it just means *you get stronger without needing to pretend anymore*.

You feel safe with yourself.

You trust your path.

You walk with intention, not anxiety.

Because when the real you rises?

You stop performing and start *being*.

You stop surviving and start *living.*

You stop shrinking and start *choosing.*

And the best part?

You're not proving anything anymore — but somehow, *you've never been more powerful.*

Reflective Exercise: Embodying the Real You

This is your moment to step fully into the version of you that no longer needs ego to feel powerful. Take a breath. Be honest. No filter, no performance — just you.

1. **What does the real, grounded version of me look and feel like?**

   (How do I carry myself, speak, think, rest, and show up when I'm not trying to impress anyone?)

2. **Where in my life am I still performing, proving, or people-pleasing — and why?**

3. **What would I do differently if I trusted that I was already enough?**

   (What would I stop chasing? What would I start allowing?)

4. **What does freedom mean to me — and how can I give that to myself today?**

5. **What daily habits or mindsets can help me stay in alignment with the real me — not the ego version of me?**

Optional Prompt:

"From this moment forward, I give myself permission to..."
Fill in the blank with the most honest, unfiltered truth you've got.

Final Closing: The Ego May Be Loud, But Truth Is Louder

Throughout this book, you've come face-to-face with the ego's games. You've seen how it hides behind pride, perfection, avoidance, and control. You've learned how it shows up in relationships, rest, success, and even love. And most importantly?

You've learned that you are not your ego.

You're the one watching it.

Questioning it.

Learning from it.

Rising above it.

This isn't about becoming perfect. This is about becoming *conscious.*

Because once you see ego for what it really is — fear in disguise — it loses its grip. And what rises in its place is the real you. The calm you. The confident you. The *unshakable* you.

Let that version lead now.

Let that version breathe.

Let that version live fully, boldly, and on purpose.

You're not here to perform. You're here to be real. And the real you? Has nothing left to prove.

This is your rise.

And it's only the beginning.

Chapter 25: When Ego Masquerades as Self-Worth

"I know my worth" isn't always rooted in truth.

Let's be real — "I know my worth" has become a catchphrase.

And sometimes, it's absolutely true.

But other times? It's the ego talking.

Loudly. Defensively.

Trying to mask insecurity as empowerment.

Because real self-worth doesn't have to announce itself.

It doesn't need to be declared in every argument.

It doesn't show up with its chest puffed out, trying to prove something.

Sometimes "I know my worth" is actually just:

"I'm scared to be vulnerable."

"I'm hurt but pretending I'm above it."

"I'm avoiding growth by calling it a standard."

The Difference Between Real Self-Worth and Ego Validation

Let's get into the real difference — because it matters. A lot of what people call "confidence" today is just the ego dressed in designer.

It's not self-worth — it's self-protection.

Real self-worth is grounded.

It's rooted in *truth*, not performance. It doesn't need to prove anything, because it already knows who it is.

- It's the kind of energy that enters the room with calm presence, not loud declarations.
- It doesn't chase validation or overexplain — it allows alignment to do the work.
- It doesn't punish people for not choosing you — it simply recognizes the mismatch and walks away with grace.
- It's the quiet "no" without a speech. The boundary without the bitterness.
- It's secure enough to love deeply without losing itself.

Self-worth moves with clarity — not control. It chooses peace — not power plays.

Ego validation, on the other hand, is loud. It's the voice in your head saying, *"They'll see. They'll regret this. I'm going to prove them wrong."*

- It thrives on being desired, chosen, praised.
- It *needs* to feel special, even if it's just to avoid feeling replaceable.
- It doesn't walk away to protect peace — it walks away to punish.
- It constantly needs to remind people (and itself) that it's above the situation.
- It uses emotional detachment as a flex, not as a boundary.

Ego isn't actually confident — it's *afraid*. And it hides that fear by trying to stay "on top."

Ego validation doesn't feel like peace — it feels like strategy. Always performing. Always defending. Always trying to look like it doesn't care.

Real self-worth says:
- "I don't need to prove myself to be respected."
- "I can have compassion and still hold boundaries."
- "I know I'm valuable — even if this person doesn't see it."
- "I'm not superior. I'm just in alignment."
- "I don't need to defend my decision to leave — I just know it's right for me."
- "Their behavior isn't a reflection of my worth — it's a reflection of theirs."

It holds truth without needing an audience. It doesn't need to be above anyone — it just needs to be *with* itself.

Ego validation says:
- "They're lucky to even have access to me."
- "I'm too good for this — next."
- "I don't need anyone. Ever."
- "They'll regret losing me."
- "I don't chase — I replace."
- "If they can't see my worth, they're beneath me."

These sound empowering, but they're often hiding *disappointment, pain, and fear of rejection.*

Ego builds armor — self-worth builds inner peace.

One walks away because it's right. The other walks away because it's *wounded*.

Self-worth walks away to protect your energy. Ego walks away to protect its pride.

And the difference isn't in the words — it's in the *intention behind them.*

When Ego Confuses Standards with Superiority

Having standards is powerful.

It shows that you know your value, and that you're not willing to settle for less than what feels aligned, respectful, and true. **But standards aren't meant to put people down — they're meant to lift *you* up.**

There's a fine line between holding high standards and using them to feed your ego.

Ego takes standards and turns them into weapons:

- To feel superior.
- To avoid intimacy.
- To stay in control.
- To never have to be vulnerable.

It goes from *"This doesn't feel aligned with who I am"* to *"I'm better than this — and better than you."*

There's a difference between saying:

"I know what I deserve."

and

"No one is good enough for me."

One comes from self-awareness and discernment. The other comes from pride and fear of being truly seen.

Sometimes people mask their pain behind phrases like:

- "My standards are just too high."
- "Nobody is on my level."
- "I intimidate people."
- "I cut people off fast — I don't have time for lessons."

But often, those aren't standards — they're *defense mechanisms.* Ego is whispering: *"Stay above it so you don't get hurt. Stay unapproachable so no one can challenge you."*

If you're using "self-worth" as a reason to:

- Look down on people
- Avoid connection
- Shut out feedback
- Keep everyone at arm's length

That's not a boundary — that's a wall. It's not confidence — it's control.

True standards *align you* with people and experiences that reflect your value — without devaluing anyone else.

They say: *"This is what I accept. This is what I need. This is what I offer."*

They don't say: *"I'm above you, and you're lucky I gave you a chance."*

Standards should elevate you — not isolate you. Self-worth should anchor you — not inflate you.

When it's real, it's not about being on top. It's about being *in tune.*

Grounded Confidence Doesn't Need to Announce Itself

You can always tell the difference.

- **Ego talks. Real confidence listens.**
  Ego needs to dominate the conversation. Grounded confidence observes, absorbs, and speaks with intention — not impulse.

- **Ego reacts. Real self-worth chooses.**
  Ego jumps to defend, explain, or clap back. Self-worth pauses. Reflects. Picks its battles — or walks away without needing one.

- **Ego needs attention. Real self-worth is at peace without it.**
  Ego thrives on being seen. Being praised. Being "known."

  Self-worth? It doesn't need to be the center of the room — because it *is* the center of its own peace.

When you're truly grounded in your worth, you don't need to say,

"I know who I am."

Because everything about you already shows it.

- The way you respond.
- The way you walk away from chaos without making a scene.
- The way you say no — not as a threat, but as a fact.
- The way you don't overexplain your value or beg for access to spaces that don't see you.

Your presence becomes your statement.
Your alignment becomes your proof.
Your clarity becomes your power.

You don't need to be loud to be powerful.

You don't need to go viral to be valuable.

You don't need to constantly declare your self-worth — you just need to *live it*.

And when you do?

People feel it.

The room shifts.

Not because you demanded attention — but because your *energy* commands respect.

Not through noise.

But through *clarity*.

Reflective Exercise: Is This Confidence or Ego?

This is about checking in with yourself — not to shame, but to *shift*. Let's get honest about where your confidence is rooted: in truth... or in the need to protect your pride.

Take a quiet moment and reflect on the following:

1. **When I set boundaries, am I doing it to protect my peace — or to prove I don't need anyone?**
2. **Do I speak about my standards with clarity and kindness... or with judgment and superiority?**
3. **Do I feel the need to constantly remind people of my worth — or am I comfortable letting my actions reflect it?**
4. **Am I walking away from situations because they're misaligned — or because my ego feels bruised?**
5. **If no one validated me, liked my post, or praised my growth... would I still feel grounded in who I am?**

Bonus prompt:

"Confidence looks like me when I..."

(What do you do, say, or embody when you're operating from grounded self-worth?)

Affirmation: I Don't Need to Prove — I Embody

1. *"I don't need to prove my worth — I embody it in how I move."*
2. *"I lead with grounded energy, not ego-driven urgency."*
3. *"My calm is not weakness — it's proof that I trust myself."*

313

Closing: Quiet Power Is Still Power

True confidence doesn't need an audience. It's not reactive. It's not defensive. It doesn't wear a crown just to feel tall.

It's quiet, steady, and undeniable.

You don't have to clap back to feel strong.

You don't have to perform your standards to feel worthy.

You don't have to be loud to be unforgettable.

You just have to be clear — and committed to being real.

Because ego needs to be seen.

But grounded confidence? It just needs to *be*.

And that's the power that actually lasts.

Chapter 26: Healing the Ego Through Inner Work

You don't destroy ego — you integrate it.

Let's start here:

Ego isn't evil.

It's not your enemy. It's not the villain. It's not some toxic part of you that needs to be "killed off."

Your ego is a *wounded protector*.

It's the part of you that learned how to survive.

How to feel safe in unsafe environments.

How to be seen when being ignored felt unbearable.

How to stay in control when everything felt chaotic. How to avoid rejection, disappointment, and shame — even if that meant building a wall around your softness.

So before you judge your ego, ask yourself:

What was it trying to protect me from?

Because ego doesn't just show up out of nowhere. It's built over time — layer by layer — to keep you from feeling powerless, rejected, unseen, or unloved. And most of the time? It started forming way before you even knew what ego *was*.

Ego Is a Response to Wounding — Not a Personality Flaw

That defensive tone? That sharpness in your voice when someone gets too close?

That urge to be right, to win the argument, to have the last word?

That obsession with being seen as accomplished, attractive, unbothered, or "above it all"?

That's not who you *really* are — that's who you had to become.

Those are not character flaws.

They're *strategies*.

Protective layers your nervous system built to keep you safe when the world didn't feel safe.

They were responses to pain, rejection, abandonment, betrayal, and unmet needs.

And at one point?

They may have actually helped you survive.

But here's the truth:

They're not rooted in your highest self.

They're not your soul — they're your shield. And shields may have helped you back then... But if you're still carrying them now, they're probably holding you back from the very connection, softness, and peace you crave.

These ego-based reactions aren't signs that you're a bad person or emotionally broken —

They're signs that there's still a younger version of you inside, whispering:

- *"If I'm not perfect, I won't be loved."*
- *"If I let people in, they'll leave me."*
- *"If I speak up, I'll be rejected."*

- *"If I don't perform, I'll disappear."*

So when your ego flares up — when you feel yourself snapping, shutting down, chasing validation, or pushing people away — It's not sabotage.
It's self-protection.
It's a part of you that learned, *a long time ago*, that safety meant control.
That connection meant proving.
That love had to be earned — or else it could vanish.

Your ego isn't trying to ruin your life.
It's trying to protect a younger part of you that never felt safe.
And until that part feels seen, nurtured, and held by *you*, your ego will keep stepping in — not because it's powerful... but because it's *scared*.
It's time to stop shaming that part of you. And start holding it with the same compassion you wish someone else had.
Because you don't heal the ego by silencing it. You heal it by asking:
"What are you afraid of?"
And then showing up — with truth, softness, and safety — to answer that fear.

Healing the Inner Child Dissolves Ego Reactions

This is where the *real* work begins.
Not the surface-level "I'm fine."

Not the spiritual performance.

Not the temporary mindset tricks.

This is the part where you stop trying to control the world around you... and start listening to the part of you that's still hurting.

You don't just tell your ego to calm down.

You *go beneath it.*

You pause in the middle of the reaction — the defensiveness, the shutting down, the proving — and you ask: **"What part of me is still carrying this pain?"**

Because behind every ego flare-up is a younger version of you who felt:

- Rejected
- Unheard
- Not good enough
- Too much or not enough
- Unloved   unless   they   performed

And the moment you start doing **inner child work** — when you *sit with that version of you*, instead of silencing or shaming them — something powerful happens:

You stop reacting — and start responding.

You're no longer just trying to protect yourself. You're *curious, aware,* and *soft enough* to choose your response instead of being ruled by your wound.

You stop needing to prove, defend, or control.

Because your worth isn't on trial anymore. That inner child finally starts to feel *seen* — not by the world, but by *you*.

You stop identifying with your pain — and start nurturing the part of you that never got what it needed.

You don't just relive your wounds — you *repair them*. With attention, compassion, patience, and presence.

You might still feel the triggers.
But now you have the emotional tools to say:
"I know where this comes from... and I choose peace instead of protection."

Healing your ego isn't about becoming "better."

It's not about being perfectly regulated, endlessly calm, or free from flaws.

It's about becoming *whole*.

It's about offering compassion — not to the polished version of you, but to the scared, scrappy, tender version of you that had to fight, hide, or perform to survive.

You don't shame that part of you.

You sit with them.

You listen to them.

You say:

- *"You're safe now."*
- *"You don't have to fight anymore."*

- *"You are worthy, even when you're soft."*

Because once your inner child feels safe...
the ego doesn't have to scream anymore.

You Don't Destroy Ego — You Integrate It

The goal isn't to silence your ego.

It's not to shame it, exile it, or pretend it's not there.

It's not to "kill the ego" like some spiritual trend would have you believe.

Because your ego?

It's not the problem — it's the protector.

And while it may not always protect you in the healthiest way, it *exists for a reason.*

It's the part of you that stepped in when you didn't feel safe.

When you didn't feel seen.

When you didn't feel worthy without a mask. And now, years later, it still shows up — not to ruin your peace, but to *guard your pain.*

But here's the truth:

- **You can't kill the ego.**
- **You shouldn't want to.**

Because even though it's wounded, **it's still part of you.** And rejecting any part of yourself only creates more fragmentation.

The real work?

The *real* flex?

Is learning how to listen to your ego… without letting it lead.

To recognize when it's speaking from fear — and gently choose a different voice.

To sit with it, honor it, but respond from your higher self — the part of you that's rooted in clarity, not chaos.

It sounds like this:
- *"I hear you."*
- *"I know you're scared."*
- *"I know you think we need to defend, prove, or protect right now."*
- *"But we're safe now."*
- *"We've grown."*
- *"And I've got this."*

That's not weakness.

That's **emotional integration.**

That's nervous system safety.

That's healing in action.

Because the truth is — you don't need to "get rid" of your ego.

You need to build a relationship with it.

You need to learn its patterns, its voice, its fears.

And then lead with love instead of letting it take over in survival mode.

Integration is the moment you stop fighting yourself — and start reuniting with the parts of you that once had to fight alone.

That's where peace comes from.

Not perfection.

Not ego death.

But *wholeness.*

Reflective Exercise: Meeting the Part of You Ego Is Protecting

This is about *listening to the part of you your ego tries to protect* — not to fix or judge it, but to understand it.

Find a quiet moment. Breathe. Drop into your body. Let this be gentle.

Ask yourself:

1. **What triggers my ego the most — criticism, rejection, being ignored, losing control, not being chosen?** *(Pick the one that stings the most.)*

2. **When I feel that trigger, what do I typically do?** *(Do I shut down? Get defensive? Lash out? Try to prove myself?)*

3. **If I imagine a younger version of myself feeling that same trigger... what does that version of me need right   now?** *(Affection? Reassurance? Safety? Validation? A hug?)*

4. **What would I say to that younger version of me if I were comforting them instead of defending myself?** *(Write the words you wish you heard back then.)*

5. **How can I start responding to myself from that place of compassion instead of ego protection?**

Optional prompt:

"Ego steps in when I feel unsafe. But my truth is..."
(Write what your grounded self wants to believe instead.)

Affirmation Drop: I Honor the Part of Me That's Still Healing

- *"I don't shame my ego — I listen to it with love."*
- *"My pain is not my identity. My healing is my power."*
- *"I give myself what I needed back then, right now."*
- *"I don't need to be perfect to be whole — I just need to be present."*

Closing: The Most Powerful Thing You Can Do Is Stay With Yourself

Your ego was never the enemy.

It was just the loudest part of you trying to keep you safe.

Now you know better.

Now you get to slow down and listen deeper.

Now you get to choose healing over defense.

Compassion over control.

Presence over performance.

You're not broken — you're layered.

And every part of you that once fought to survive... deserves to rest now.

You don't have to fight anymore.

You just have to stay with yourself.

That's what integration looks like.

That's what healing sounds like.

This is how you rise — not by rejecting the ego... but by holding the part of you it's been trying to protect.

And now? You've got you.

Conclusion: A New Way of Thinking

Ego doesn't have to be your downfall.

It doesn't have to keep sabotaging your relationships, blocking your growth, or trapping you in toxic patterns that feel too familiar.

Because now?

You see it.

You know how ego works.

How it twists the truth just enough to protect your pride. How it confuses reaction for power, control for confidence, silence for strength.

You've seen how it feeds on validation, fuels unnecessary conflict, and fears anything that challenges it. You've seen how it keeps you defensive, disconnected, and stuck in cycles that feel safe—but aren't serving you.

And now that you know the game...

You don't have to keep playing it.

The Power of Self-Awareness, Humility, and Inner Confidence

Mastering ego isn't about pretending you don't have one. It's about recognizing when it shows up—and choosing *not* to let it lead.

It's choosing:

Self-awareness over blind reaction.

Humility over arrogance.

Curiosity over defensiveness.

Inner confidence over needing to be seen, validated, or agreed with.

Because real power isn't loud.

It's steady.

Grounded. Calm. Unshakable.

It doesn't rush to defend itself—because it knows who it is.

True success isn't about being above others. It's about rising above the parts of yourself that try to keep you small.

True confidence isn't about being the loudest in the room. It's being so secure in who you are... you no longer need to convince anyone else.

That's the shift.

That's the evolution.

That's the new way of thinking.

A Final Challenge: Who's in Control—You or Your Ego?

From this moment on, life won't suddenly get easier.

But *you'll move differently.*

You'll notice more. Respond better. Choose differently.

Because now, every interaction... every emotion... every decision... comes with a choice:

Will I let my ego take over—or will I choose a higher response?

Will I react out of habit—or pause, breathe, and respond from truth?

Will I chase validation—or root into the knowing that I am already enough?

The difference between people who evolve and people who stay stuck?

Who wins that battle.

Every time.

So here's your challenge—the one that matters most:

Will you let your ego control you?

Or will you become the one in control?

Because the truth is:

Your ego doesn't get the final say anymore.

You do.

And now?

You're ready.

Real-Life Case Studies: Relatable Examples of Ego in Action

Talking about ego is one thing—but *seeing* how it actually shows up in real life? That's what makes the message *stick*.

Ego isn't always loud or obvious.

Sometimes, it sounds like confidence...

Sometimes, it hides behind "boundaries," "logic," or even "love." And sometimes, it's so woven into your habits, your friendships, your parenting, or your leadership that you don't even realize it's there—until it's too late.

That's why these real-life case studies matter.

They aren't abstract theories.

They're *realistic, everyday situations*—the kind you've either lived, witnessed, or been affected by.

These stories put a mirror in front of you.

Not to shame you, but to show you what ego looks like *in action*... before it silently sabotages your life.

In each example, you'll see the subtle ways ego drives people to:

- Destroy good relationships
- Miss out on life-changing opportunities
- Push away love
- Confuse pride for power
- And stay stuck—while blaming everyone else

These aren't just stories.

They're lessons.

Each one is a wake-up call.

Each one is an invitation to *catch yourself sooner,* shift your perspective, and choose growth over pride.

Because once you see ego clearly...

You can stop letting it control you—and finally start living from a place of truth, peace, and real power.

1. The Frenemy: Hyping You Up While Secretly Hoping You Fail

Meet Sarah. She's ambitious, creative, and ready to make some big changes in her life. But she's also navigating uncertainty, self-doubt, and a lot of emotional decisions.

Enter Jessica—her "ride or die." The friend who always hypes her up...

Or at least, that's what it *looks* like on the surface.

- "You're way too smart for that job. Just quit—don't let them play you."
- "Block him, sis. Closure is overrated."
- "Girl, life is short—just book the trip, buy the bag. You've earned it."

At first, it feels like support. Sarah feels seen, validated, and "empowered."

But in reality? Jessica isn't helping her level up—she's helping her crash.

Every time Sarah feels unsure, Jessica's right there—pushing her toward the most impulsive, emotionally charged decision. Not with guidance. Not with love. But with *ego-fueled encouragement.*

And slowly, things unravel.

- Sarah quits her job with no backup, thinking she'll figure it out later—but later never comes.
- She ghosts people she had real relationships with instead of facing uncomfortable but necessary conversations.
- She spends recklessly to soothe the chaos, chasing short-term highs to avoid long-term discipline.

And Jessica?

She's still in the same place.

Stable, careful, and *always watching*—cheering people into chaos from the sidelines while never taking the leap herself.

Why?

Because ego thrives on comparison.

And some people will hype you up—not to help you grow—but to watch you fall and feel better about staying small.

Moral of the Story:

Not everyone who hypes you up is truly rooting for you.

Some people feed your ego, not your growth.

They mask sabotage as support.

They dress projection up as empowerment.

And they love to see you "be bold" as long as it doesn't end in you actually succeeding.

Real support checks you, holds you accountable, and challenges you to think before you leap.

It's not about being a dream-killer.

It's about being a *reality-checker*—with love.

Because the people who *truly* want to see you win?

They won't just cheer for you when it's easy.

They'll guide you when it's hard—and tell you the truth when your ego is getting in the way.

2. The Know-It-All Leader: Ignoring Advice Until It's Too Late

Meet David. He started with nothing but a big idea and a dream—and it worked.

He launched a small business that blew up fast. In the early days, he was hungry. Curious. Open.

He asked questions. Took advice. Leaned on his team. And that's exactly what made his business grow.

But then? Success happened.

And slowly... ego took the wheel.

- David stopped listening to feedback—especially if it came from someone "less experienced."
- He started micromanaging everything, thinking no one could do it as well as he could.
- He shut down new ideas with the classic line: *"I know what I'm doing."*

At first, it looked like confidence.

But it was pride in disguise.

And his team started to feel it.

They went from feeling *valued* to feeling *managed*. From being part of the vision... to just executing his control.

Then came the resignations.

One by one, his most talented employees left.

Innovation slowed down. Morale dropped. The culture shifted. And while David was busy defending his way of doing things, his competitors were adapting, evolving—and winning.

The worst part?

David didn't fail because he lacked skill or talent.

He failed because he stopped learning.

He confused experience with wisdom—and missed the fact that *true leadership* is rooted in humility.

Moral of the Story:

The moment you stop being coachable, you stop growing.

Ego tricks people into thinking they've already arrived.

That they've got it all figured out.

That success is proof they no longer need help, feedback, or fresh ideas.

But success without humility is a setup for stagnation. You can't lead from a place of control. You lead from a place of *trust, curiosity, and adaptability.*

Because staying on top isn't about *knowing everything.* It's about knowing you *never will*—and choosing to grow anyway.

3. The Person Who Blames Everything Else Instead of Looking Inward

Meet Jason.

On the surface, he seems like someone who just has "bad luck." Nothing ever goes his way—at least, that's what *he* tells himself.

Every area of his life feels like a struggle.

Dating? A mess.

Career? Stagnant.

Friendships? Drifting.

But ask Jason why, and he's got an explanation for *everything*—as long as the problem isn't him.

- "Women are the problem. They're all the same."
- "I'm a Scorpio—what do you expect? I can't help how I am."
- "The system's rigged. People like me never get a fair shot."
- "That job? Probably went to someone who had connections."
- "My friend's just being sensitive. They know how I talk."

Anytime someone challenges him, even gently, his ego jumps out to defend, deflect, and distract.

He can't see that the real issue isn't the world around him—it's the patterns *within* him.

And while everyone else is evolving, reflecting, and moving forward—Jason stays exactly where he is:

- Same complaints.
- Same insecurities.
- Same defensiveness.
- Same results.

Because the more you blame, the less you grow. And ego *loves* blame—it keeps you comfortable in your own delusion.

Moral of the Story:
Ego will always try to convince you that the world is the problem.

It'll hand you excuses dressed as reasons.

It'll protect your pride at the expense of your progress.

It'll block the lesson just to save face.

But growth?

That starts the moment you look in the mirror and say,

"Maybe it's me. And maybe that's okay—because I can change."

**The power move isn't blaming.

It's reflecting.

It's taking accountability.

It's being honest enough with yourself to ask:

What's the common denominator in my patterns?

And brave enough to answer: *Me.*

And wise enough to follow that with: *Let me do better."*

4. The Humble Person Who Thrives: Learning, Growing, and Leveling Up

Meet Rachel.

She's not the loudest in the room.

She's not always the most confident.

But she's the one people go to for wisdom, consistency, and real results.

Why? Because Rachel doesn't let ego run the show.

- When someone gives her feedback—even if it stings—she *listens.*

- When she gets called out, she doesn't spiral into defensiveness—she reflects.

- She doesn't surround herself with people who hype her up no matter what. She surrounds herself with people who challenge her to *get better*.

She's not perfect.

Her ego still shows up—because it always will.

But instead of letting it speak for her, she slows down and asks:

- *"What can I learn from this?"*
- *"Am I reacting out of pride or responding with wisdom?"*
- *"Is this about them—or something I need to look at in myself?"*

She's not afraid to be wrong.

She's afraid of staying the same.

And that mindset? That's her *superpower*.

What Happens?

- She gets promoted while others complain.
- She builds deep, drama-free relationships rooted in trust—not ego.
- She makes smarter choices, both personally and professionally, because her decisions aren't based on emotion—they're based on *clarity*.

Rachel thrives—not because she's the smartest, the loudest, or the flashiest—

but because she's **humble enough to grow.**

Moral of the Story:

The people who win long-term aren't the ones with the biggest egos.

They're the ones with the biggest willingness to *learn*.

To adjust.

To take accountability.

To stay grounded while everyone else is trying to look impressive.

Ego screams, "I'm already great!"

Wisdom whispers, "I'm just getting started."

And that's the difference.

More Real-Life Case Studies: Ego in Action

These next ones go even deeper—exposing how ego hides, reacts, manipulates, and *blocks growth* in every area of life.

This time, we're not just scratching the surface.

We're pulling back the layers.

These examples are designed to trigger *every perspective*—the boss, the lover, the friend, the parent, the dreamer, the one who swears "that's not me" but lowkey *knows it is*.

Because here's the truth:

Ego doesn't discriminate.

It shows up whether you're rich or struggling.

Male or female. Confident or insecure. Young or seasoned.

You don't have to be loud or arrogant to have an ego problem.

Sometimes, ego *whispers quietly in your blind spots,* and that's even more dangerous.

These case studies are for *everyone*—and if you're brave enough to read with honesty, you'll start to notice your own patterns in the people on these pages.

So buckle up.

No more hiding behind good intentions or "that's just how I am."

This is where ego gets exposed—and truth takes the wheel.

5. The Woman Who Ruins Her Own Relationship Because of Ego

Meet Vanessa.

She's been dating Mike for two years.

On paper, he's everything she's ever wanted—loyal, supportive, emotionally available.

He communicates. He shows up. He *chooses* her.

And at first, it's amazing.

But then?

Vanessa's ego starts to whisper...

- *"If he really loved you, he'd text you back immediately."*
- *"If he cared, he'd try harder to win you over every day."*
- *"If he's not chasing you, maybe he's losing interest."*

Instead of trusting the peace, she starts craving chaos. Not because she doesn't love him—but because ego *needs proof.*

And so it begins:

- She tests him constantly. If he takes too long to reply, she accuses him of not caring.

- She creates drama when things are too calm—because conflict feels like passion, and peace feels unfamiliar.
- She doesn't apologize. Even when she knows she's wrong, she spins it into *"You triggered me."*
- Every disagreement becomes a loyalty test.
- Every conversation becomes a power struggle.

Mike tries. Over and over.

But no matter how consistent he is, how many times he explains himself, or how much love he gives—it's never enough.

Because she's not fighting *with* him.

She's fighting the fear within her—and letting ego lead the way.

What Happens?

Eventually, Mike reaches his limit.

Not because he stopped loving her.

But because love shouldn't feel like a never-ending exam.

He walks away—quietly, respectfully, and completely.

And Vanessa?

Instead of taking accountability, she clings to the same narrative:

"Men always leave."

"He wasn't strong enough to handle me."

"He gave up."

But deep down, a part of her knows:

He didn't leave because of who she was—he left because of who her ego wouldn't let her become.

Moral of the Story:

Testing someone until they break isn't love—it's ego trying to control the outcome.

Constant reassurance isn't connection—it's insecurity in disguise.

Pushing someone away just to see if they'll come back isn't romantic—it's manipulation rooted in fear.

If you can't meet someone halfway, if you won't own your part, if you constantly need to *win* the argument instead of resolve it...

Don't be surprised when the person you're fighting to "keep" chooses to walk away.

Because real love doesn't live where ego takes up all the space.

6. The Self-Sabotaging Employee: Ego Kills Opportunity

Meet James.

He's smart. Skilled. Naturally talented.

But in his mind, he's underappreciated.

No one at work "sees his value."

No one gives him the recognition he "deserves."

At least, that's what his ego keeps telling him.

And because of that belief, his actions start to shift:

- When his boss gives him feedback, he takes it personally—like it's an insult instead of guidance.
- When he's overwhelmed, he refuses to ask for help— because to him, needing help = weakness.

- He constantly talks about how he *should* be further ahead—but does nothing to actually *get* there.

Then one day, a younger coworker—someone newer, someone quieter, someone who *actually listens*—gets promoted before him.

And instead of asking:

"What did they do differently?"

"How can I improve?"

He spirals into resentment.

- "It's just favoritism."
- "I've been here longer—I earned that spot."
- "They   got   lucky."

From there, things only get worse.

He stops putting in effort.

He checks out emotionally.

He starts doing the bare minimum—because deep down, he's convinced he's being wronged.

But his manager isn't blind—they see it.

They notice the shift in attitude, the passive aggression, the resistance to growth.

And when the *next* big opportunity comes around? James isn't even in the conversation.

What Happens?

James doesn't get passed over because of politics, favoritism, or bad luck.

He gets passed over because of *ego*.

340

He chose pride over progress.

Validation over humility.

And in doing so, he sabotaged the very thing he claimed to want.

Moral of the Story:

If you're not getting the results you want, check your ego before blaming everything else.

- Are you putting in the work, or just expecting the reward?
- Are you open to feedback, or only praise?
- Are you showing up with growth energy—or entitlement?

Because sometimes, the only thing standing between you and success...

is you.

7. The Jealous Friend Who Secretly Hopes You Fail

Meet Brianna and Tasha.

They've been best friends since high school—thick as thieves, inseparable, always in sync.

But as they got older, their lives started to take different paths.

Tasha started glowing up.

She began putting herself first.

She hit the gym, landed a dream job, and met a man who actually treated her right.

Brianna smiled on the outside—but on the inside? Ego was eating her alive.

Instead of celebrating her friend's wins, her pride started whispering:

- *"Why her, not me?"*
- *"She doesn't even know how good she has it."*
- *"It won't last anyway."*

And it showed.

- She threw subtle shade: "Must be nice to have everything handed to you."
- She downplayed Tasha's accomplishments: "Yeah, but you just got lucky."
- She planted seeds of doubt: "He seems too good to be true. Be careful."

At first, Tasha tried to overlook it.
But over time, she couldn't ignore the shift.

Every time she shared something positive, Brianna found a way to make it feel *small, suspicious,* or *self-centered.*

The vibe went from supportive to *competitive.*

From celebratory to *heavy.*

From real to *resentful.*

What Happens?

Tasha starts pulling back.

Not because she thinks she's better... but because she feels *unseen.*

And when she finally distances herself, Brianna doesn't self-reflect.

She doesn't ask, *"Was I showing up as a real friend?"*

Instead, ego kicks in again:

- "She changed."
- "She thinks she's too good for me now."
- "Whatever, she was never real anyway."

But the truth?

Tasha didn't leave Brianna behind.

Brianna's ego pushed her away.

Moral of the Story:

If you can't clap for your friends, don't expect the universe to hand you your own wins.

Jealousy disguised as concern is still jealousy. Backhanded compliments are still rooted in competition. And constantly making someone else's success about *you*? That's not friendship—that's ego.

Real friends don't compete. They support.

They uplift. They celebrate each other—even when they're still waiting on their own breakthrough.

Because when your heart is open, your moment always comes.

But when your ego's in control, you'll miss your blessings while hating on someone else's.

8. The Man Who Thinks Success Means He's Above Everyone

Meet Marcus.

He came from humble beginnings.

Worked hard.

Climbed out of struggle.

And now? He's *made it.*

- He's got money.
- He's got influence.
- He's got respect—at least on the surface.

At first, he stayed grounded.

He was humble, generous, and hungry to learn more.

But over time, ego crept in—and completely rewired his mindset.

- He started looking down on people who hadn't "made it" yet.
- He stopped listening to anyone who didn't praise him.
- He forgot the hustle it took to get here—and started mocking people who were still in the process.

Instead of being a mentor, he became a gatekeeper.

Instead of giving back, he hoarded praise.

And instead of growing with his success, he let ego *stunt* it.

Then One Day... It Starts to Slip.

Marcus gets too comfortable.

He assumes the money will always flow.

The status will always stay.

The people around him will never leave.

So he stops learning.

He rejects feedback.

He coasts on past wins instead of planning for future ones.

And while he's looking down on others...

Someone else is leveling up with *humility, hunger, and vision.*

- His competition evolves faster.
- His business starts crumbling from the inside.
- The yes-men he surrounded himself with? They disappear the moment things get hard.

And just like that...

He's back where he started.

Not because he wasn't talented.

Not because the world turned on him.

But because **his ego stopped him from evolving.**

Moral of the Story:

Success isn't a finish line—it's a mindset.

It's not about reaching the top once.

It's about *staying* there—ethically, humbly, and with growth.

Ego will tell you, *"You're better than them."*

Wisdom will remind you, *"You were them."*

Ego will say, *"You've arrived."*

But real success says, *"There's still more to learn."*

Because the second you think you've "made it"?

You stop *making* it.

And the fall?

It's never about talent.

It's about mindset.

9. The Two Fake Supporters: When Men Pretend to Be Happy for Each Other

Meet Alex and Jordan.

They've been close since college—bonded over big dreams, ambition, and the grind.

They talk about success, leveling up, building empires.

But underneath all that hype?

Their friendship is built more on comparison than connection.

It's not *genuine support*—it's a scoreboard.

When Alex gets a promotion at a top firm, Jordan texts: "Bro! That's huge, proud of you!"

But in his head, he's spiraling:

- *"He's not even that smart…"*
- *"He just got lucky. Probably kissed up to the right people."*
- *"Let's see how long he lasts."*

When Jordan's business finally starts thriving, Alex comments: "Boss moves! Big money!"

But his words come wrapped in shade:

- "Hope you can keep it up. Most businesses flop after the first year."
- "Man, don't forget about us little people now that you're balling."
- "Must be nice to have that kind of luck."

They both smile, cheer, and post the fire emojis.

But deep down?

Every win feels like a loss.

Every "congrats" is laced with ego.

Every milestone is a threat—not an inspiration.

What Happens?

Over time, the fake support turns toxic:

- Alex stops replying when Jordan shares good news.
- Jordan starts over-explaining his success, trying to justify it instead of enjoying it.
- The jokes turn sharp. The compliments feel forced. The energy shifts from brotherhood to cold competition.

Neither one will admit it out loud, but they both start hoping the other slips up.

Because ego would rather see someone fail than feel like it's falling behind.

Then one day, Jordan says something slick that cuts too deep—and Alex finally sees it for what it is:

This was never a friendship.

It was an ego battle in disguise.

Moral of the Story:

If your "support" is rooted in jealousy, shade, or competition—you're not a friend.

You're a silent rival.

True support isn't conditional.

It's not based on who's ahead.

It's not about keeping score or silently hoping for someone to fall just so you can feel better.

Real friends celebrate wins even when they're behind. Because love doesn't flinch when someone else rises. Only ego does.

10. The Parent Who Resents Their Own Success (But Won't Admit It)

Meet Robert.

He grew up with nothing—working long hours as a teen, scraping by, sacrificing his own childhood just to survive. Every decision he made came from survival mode. And now? He's built a life his son, Daniel, never had to struggle for.

Daniel has safety.

Stability.

Opportunities Robert never even dreamed of.

And on the surface, Robert is proud.

He *says* he worked this hard so Daniel wouldn't have to suffer the way he did.

But deep down?

He resents it.

Not out of hatred—but out of a complex emotional conflict he's never dealt with.

- When Daniel expresses his stress, Robert says, *"Stressed about what? You have everything."*
- When Daniel talks about his challenges, Robert shrugs, *"You kids wouldn't last a day in my shoes."*

- When Daniel tries to set a boundary, Robert hears it as *disrespect,* not maturity.

Because to Robert, **respect is earned through struggle.**
And if his son hasn't suffered like he did?
His ego tells him: *"Then he doesn't get to feel what I feel."*

What Happens?

Daniel slowly shuts down.

- He stops opening up.
- He stops asking for advice.
- He stops trying to prove himself—because *what's the point?*

Robert unknowingly sends the message:
"Unless your pain looks like mine, it doesn't count."
"Unless you've struggled like me, you haven't earned your voice."
"Unless you suffer, your emotions are weakness—not real problems."
Over time, both sides grow resentful.

- Robert feels unappreciated.
- Daniel feels unseen.
- The bond breaks—not from lack of love, but from lack of *understanding.*

The Deeper Truth

Here's the crazy part:
Robert worked his whole life to give his child a better path—then resents him for not having to crawl through the mud.

Why? Because somewhere along the way, he tied his *self-worth* to suffering.

- Struggle became his identity.
- Pain became his proof of value.
- Hardship became the lens through which he measured *everything*.

So when he sees his child thriving without that same pain?
It shakes him.
It messes with his identity.
And without realizing it... **he starts punishing his child for the very success he helped create.**

Moral of the Story:

Just because you struggled doesn't mean your child has to. And just because their pain looks different doesn't mean it's not *real*.

Being older doesn't automatically make you right. Your child is a person—not just an extension of your past. And if you don't listen to them? One day, they'll stop talking.

And that's not rebellion.

That's heartbreak.

Generational trauma doesn't always look like abuse.

Sometimes, it sounds like "tough love."

Sometimes, it feels like constant invalidation.

And sometimes, it's just unhealed pain wearing the mask of "I just want what's best for you."

The real goal was always to give your children a better life. So don't punish them for living it.

Reminders to Revisit

For the moments you forget who's really in charge.

You are not your ego.

You are the one observing it. You always have a choice.

The loudest voice isn't always the wisest.

Ego screams. Truth speaks. Listen deeper.

> **Defensiveness is a mirror, not a weapon.**
>
> Ask yourself: *What am I protecting right now?*
>
> **Proving your worth is exhausting — embodying it is magnetic.**

Stop performing. Start aligning.

> **If it's peace you want, you have to stop choosing chaos.**

You don't have to attend every argument you're invited to.

> **You don't have to be perfect to be powerful.**

The real flex is knowing when to pause, own it, and grow.

> **The ego is not the enemy — but it's not the leader either.**

Let it ride with you, not drive you.

> **The most secure people move quietly.**
>
> Stillness is power. So is softness. So is walking away without a show.
>
> **The real you doesn't need to be louder — just clearer.**

Lead with clarity, not control.

> **Healing isn't a performance.**
>
> You don't have to be fully healed to be deeply worthy. Show up anyway.

> Whenever you forget — come back here.
> The ego might flare.

The fear might return.

But now, you *know better.*

And when you know better — you lead differently.

You're not at war with yourself anymore.

You're building trust with the real you.

That's the work.

That's the shift.

That's the rise.

The "Ego Check" Self-Contract

A conscious commitment to lead with truth, not ego.

You've done the work. You've faced the ego, softened the armor, and seen the truth underneath.

Now it's time to take ownership of your growth — not just in theory, but in action.

This is your moment to get clear on who you no longer want to be...

and who you're choosing to become.

Take your time with this.

Be raw. Be honest. No fluff.

This isn't about writing what sounds evolved — it's about writing what feels *real*.

Step 1: Identify the Patterns

What are the ego patterns you now recognize in yourself? (List all that apply, and feel free to elaborate.)

"When I'm in ego, I tend to..."

→ *(Ex: Shut down emotionally, talk over people, need constant validation, cut people off too quickly, become defensive, overwork, compare myself, etc.)*

What is your ego usually trying to protect you from?

→ *(Ex: Being abandoned, being wrong, being judged, being seen as weak, being hurt again, being overlooked...)*

Step 2: Recognize the Shift

How do you feel when you're grounded in truth — not ego?

→ *(Ex: Peaceful, present, powerful, clear, soft, calm, whole, free...)*

What does the real you — the grounded, authentic you — look and feel like in action?

→ *(How do you speak? What do you no longer tolerate? What boundaries do you hold? How do you carry yourself?)*

Step 3: Define Your New Standard

Answer these with truth and clarity:

1. **I no longer need to prove...**
2. **I no longer shrink to avoid...**
3. **I no longer perform in order to...**
4. **I am learning to choose...**
5. **I want to lead my life with...**

Step 4: Conscious Commitments

Write 3 to 5 clear commitments to yourself that you will return to whenever your ego tries to take over.

These can be simple or deep — as long as they're honest.

Going forward, I commit to...

→ *(Examples: Speaking with compassion. Walking away without making a scene. Asking what's underneath my anger. Listening before defending. Taking a breath before reacting. Reminding myself I am safe even when I feel triggered.)*

Step 5: Write Your Ego A Letter (Optional, but powerful)

If you're feeling it, write a short letter directly to your ego.

You can say things like:

"Thank you for protecting me when I didn't know how."

"I don't hate you. I'm just ready to lead now."

"You don't have to disappear — but you don't get to run the show anymore."

"I'll listen to you, but I'll respond from my truth."

This is closure. Integration. Ownership.

Step 6: Your Self-Worth Contract

Write this by hand — or print and sign it. Make it real.

I am no longer living from fear, pride, or protection.

I am grounded in truth, and I trust myself to lead.

I know I will still feel triggered, insecure, and unsure at times — but I will no longer let ego control my voice, my choices, or my worth.

I am not my past. I am not my patterns.

I am the one creating my future — with clarity, intention, and softness.

I do not have to be perfect. I just have to keep showing up as *me*.

This is my conscious commitment to return to my power — not my ego.

Signed: _____

Date: _____

Keep this somewhere sacred — revisit it when old patterns resurface.

This isn't the end.

It's the beginning of the real you leading your life — not from defense, but from *alignment*.

Because the ego might still get loud...

But your truth? Will always be louder.

The Ego Exposure Exercise

Do something you usually avoid because of fear of how you'll be perceived.

Why it works:

The ego thrives on image management. It constantly asks, *"How do I look?"* or *"Will this make me seem weak, weird, or less than?"*

So the fastest way to disarm it?

Intentionally do something that makes your ego uncomfortable — and observe what comes up without editing yourself.

Examples (Pick One or Create Your Own):

- Post a photo or video without filters, perfect lighting, or a curated caption.
- Wear an outfit you love but usually feel "too much" or "not enough" in.
- Let someone see you cry — without apologizing for it.
- Admit you're wrong in a conversation *without explaining why you were kind of right.*
- Tell someone you appreciate or admire them *without trying to sound cool or casual.*
- Ask for help where you normally suffer in silence.
- Speak about your accomplishments out loud without self-deprecating to soften the blow.
- Be silent in a moment where your ego would normally jump in to defend or explain.

Reflection Questions (Do Afterward):
1. What was my ego afraid would happen if I did this?
2. What feelings came up before, during, and after?
3. What did I learn about myself — and what still needs healing?
4. Did I survive it? Did it actually go the way my ego feared?
5. What did it feel like to be seen without the shield?

Why This Is Powerful:

This activity puts you face-to-face with your most subtle ego habits — the ones you *live in* daily without even realizing. It forces you to choose **authenticity over image, connection over control,** and **growth over performance** — not in theory, but in *real time.*

It doesn't just build confidence.

It builds **ego awareness** through *embodied experience* — and that's where the real rewiring happens.

The Trigger Translation Guide
What You're Feeling & What It's Trying to Teach You

Sometimes emotions hit hard and fast, and the ego jumps in to protect us. But behind every emotional trigger is a message. This is your quick reference guide—to help you pause, identify what's really going on underneath, and gently guide yourself back to center.

Use this whenever you feel off, overwhelmed, or just need clarity in the moment.

What Your Triggers Mean

A quick guide to understanding what your emotions are trying to tell you.

- **Anger** tells us when a fundamental need is being ignored or dismissed.
- **Shame** invites us to practice giving ourselves acceptance and love.
- **Jealousy** shows us what we want for ourselves and where we feel "less than."
- **Judgment** or criticism of others shows us where we judge ourselves.
- **Depression** shows us when our soul is not being nourished by the way we're living.
- **Overwhelm** invites us to pause and release the things we don't need to do.
- **Exhaustion** invites us to put boundaries in place to stop us from over-functioning.

- **Dissociation** tells us we're feeling unsafe and invites us to return to our body and ground.
- **Anxiety** reminds us we're focused on what we can't control and invites us to return to the present.
- **Envy** highlights our unspoken desires and where we feel disconnected from possibility.
- **Resentment** reveals where we've abandoned ourselves or stayed silent for too long.
- **Loneliness** shows us where we're disconnected—from others or from ourselves
- **Guilt** can point to a value misalignment or a need for self-forgiveness.
- **Fear** shows us where we don't feel safe—and invites us to question if the danger is real or perceived.
- **Frustration** tells us something isn't working and it's time to reassess or pivot.
- **Insecurity** reveals where we're seeking external validation instead of internal grounding.
- **Bitterness** shows us where pain hasn't been acknowledged or healed.
- **Disappointment** invites us to realign our expectations and reconnect with what truly matters.
- **Confusion** means we need stillness—not more input—to find clarity.

A closing mantra or affirmation

Something simple you repeat when you feel triggered or overwhelmed.

Examples:

- *"This feeling is not who I am—it's something I'm moving through."*
- *"I honor what I feel, but I am not controlled by it."*
- *"Pause. Breathe. Feel. Heal."*

Reminder:

Recognizing a trigger is already growth, and healing takes time.

You won't always catch it in the moment, and that's okay. This isn't about being perfect—it's about being honest with yourself, little by little. Every trigger is a lesson. Every moment is a chance to shift.

Space to reflect:

Today I was triggered by:

What it was trying to show me:

How I responded (and how I'd like to respond next time):

Acknowledgments

This book was born from experience—every lesson, obstacle, and moment of growth that pushed me to see life beyond the surface.

To those who challenged my thinking, asked the tough questions, or shared wisdom at just the right time—thank you. You helped shape the clarity behind these words.

To my friends and family—your love, patience, and belief in me never went unnoticed. I'm grateful for every moment you stood by me.

To my readers—thank you for choosing this book. I hope it brings you the insight, strength, and self-mastery you need to rise above what no longer serves you. I love every one of you.

And to the version of me that refused to give up—thank you for pushing through, for wanting better, and for believing there was more. This book is for you.

About the Author

Bridgette is an author and creative with a passion for personal growth, deep conversations, and cutting through the noise to uncover the truth. With an innate ability to understand people and what truly drives them, her writing is both insightful and grounded—designed to wake you up, not lull you into comfort.

She believes life is about understanding yourself, taking action, and maintaining a clear perspective—a philosophy that inspired Living With Purpose and continues through Your Ego Is Your Biggest Downfall. Her work helps readers break free from overthinking, align with their own truth, and move forward with clarity and confidence.

When she's not writing, Bridgette is exploring bold ideas, creating meaningful content, and fully embracing the journey of constant growth.

Bridgette doesn't sugarcoat life—she breaks it down, calls it out, and helps you rise above it. A truth-teller at heart and a creator with purpose, she's known for transforming deep thoughts into powerful wake-up calls. Her words challenge the ego, inspire action, and remind you who the hell you are—beneath the noise, the fear, and the façade.

Connect with Bridgette:
@heyqueenbrii on TikTok, Instagram, and X

To stay connected, visit www.ponsveritas.com and subscribe for updates, new releases, exclusive downloads, and a steady dose of truth you won't find anywhere else.